IF IT DOESN'T CHALLENGE YOU, IT DOESN'T CHANGE YOU.

All rights reserved. No part of this book may be reproduced in any form on or by electronic or mechanical means, including information storage and retrieval systems, without permission in writing from the publisher, except by a reviewer who may quote brief passages in a review.

NOT AVAILABLE FOR RESALE.

Copyright © 2020 Cannonball Ventures, LLC

Cover Design: Lindsey Kaney, LK Design and Photography

Video Content Contributors:

Brent Scott | Jake Dixon | Jennifer Taylor | Jennifer Henry | Leonna Weiss | Mark Simpson | Nathan Daniel

www.TLRNation.com

LETTER FROM THE FOUNDER

To our partners, thank you for believing in the vision, mission, and belief system of The Locker Room. Our commitment is to provide you with the tools, methods, and resources necessary to build a profitable and sustainable real estate business that funds your perfect life.

The Locker Room specializes in helping agents who are in their first two years of the business or currently sell 24 or fewer homes per year and want to reach the next level of success. We built our vision on the facts which claim 97% of the National Association of Realtors sell 24 or fewer homes per year, making only 3% who are reasonably able to afford most coaching programs in today's industry. When you combine this statistic with over 80% of new agents not making it past their first two years in the business, it has created a need and The Locker Room has created the solution. We're not willing to stand on the sidelines with an accepting attitude. It's time to get our jerseys dirty and stand up against the industry "norm" by providing proven solutions that have impacted thousands of agents and coaches all across the Nation who are part of The Locker Room Nation.

We know real estate is a challenging business. We know it's not what reality TV shows lead you to believe. We also recognize most agents are struggling to launch their real estate careers. The Locker Room refuses to let price be the determining factor when it comes to your ability to receive world-class coaching, training, and support. For this reason, we have put together the "Agent T.R.A.C.K." program just for you! Top real estate coaching minds from across the country have collaborated to create a duplicatable 12-week curriculum. Our program balances intense productivity specific actions combined with video training modules to accompany each week and each new lesson.

We have broken the 12-week curriculum down into four primary components, each representing a 3-week time frame: Foundation, Skills, Systems, & Achievement. It is essential to play all in when utilizing T.R.A.C.K. You must be committed to the process associated with achieving success. Often, the pathway to success can be tedious, mundane, and repetitious. You must accept the boredom associated with success and reaching mastery! No one said this was going to be easy, but I can assure you it's worth it on the other side. You will be met with a lot of temptations such as pulling up short on your contacts, throwing in the towel after a few weeks, or treating the entire program as if it were a menu instead of a proven model. Commitment means doing what you said you were going to do, long after the feeling and emotion in which you said it has passed. There's a reason you're here. Stay focused on your goals and your BIG WHY, and let the haters be your motivators. You haven't come this far only to come this far. Be consistent, stay committed, and stand up for the greatness you have within you, instead of taking a stance for any fear or limiting beliefs you may have.

Real estate is a contact sport, so it's time to get your jersey dirty and go out and build relationships. You can create a referral-based business that is sustainable over the long term, regardless of market conditions.

Health, Wealth, and Happiness

Jake Dixon
The Locker Room Founder/CEO

WHAT TO EXPECT

Agent T.R.A.C.K. consists of four sections: **Foundation, Skills, Systems, & Achievement**. Each section, split up into three weeks of activities, focuses on that sections' objective. Every week contains a list of activities that builds off of the previous week, the resources to use to complete those activities, a planner page to time block your activities, and a tracking sheet to track what you have accomplished.

FOUNDATION	SKILLS	SYSTEMS	ACHIEVEMENT
In the Foundation section, you will have clarity around your goals, establish the activities it will take to achieve those goals, and know how to protect your time, so your calendar reflects your goals.	At the end of the Skills section you will be on the path towards mastery and fully equipped with the skills and tools required to identify blind spots and convert business at a high level.	By the end of the Systems section, you will have built and refined your systems and be working towards higher efficiency and effectiveness so you can work smarter, not just harder	In the Achievement, you will be able to clearly articulate your story which will allow you to create a referral-based business and create more meaningful relationships, which leads to more business and increased conversion rates.

ACTIVITIES

It is essential to provide context around the activities we have challenged you to complete throughout T.R.A.C.K. Our team chooses every activity with mathematical precision based on consistently tracking agent activities for years and recording the proven results. The specifically designed activities within T.R.A.C.K. increase your database by over 250 people within a 12-week time frame and make a minimum of 600 meaningful contacts with people about real estate. The result? Our data suggests a 50:1 ratio when analyzing contacts that result in a new piece of business, such as a listing taken or a new buyer agreement signed. Given the national average of $250,000 sales price and assuming an average gross commission of $7,500, we can safely say if you remain consistent with the T.R.A.C.K. program you will have roughly 12 new pieces of business under contract within the 12-week time frame. Resulting in approximately $90,000 of agent commissions earned.

T.R.A.C.K. is not your average hyped-up program that lacks years of testing and results. Our system is proven, and our data complete. We've taken a mathematical approach because we believe numbers are the language of business and are unbiased and unemotional. Numbers do not lie, and if you commit to treating this seriously, there is no reason you won't be able to achieve results similar to what is mentioned above. Of course, we cannot guarantee results because it is up to you and your ability to connect and convert authentically. Our strategy is not guesswork. Everything done throughout this program is very intentional and carefully thought through to put you in the best position for success.

Please note that each week has its own set of activities and milestones for you to complete. We've provided a weekly planner for you to utilize to make sure your calendar reflects your priorities. Additionally, it is vitally important that you reference the appendix for any accompanying documents that may play a role in the activities of the week. You need to make a high priority to watch each video module that corresponds with the training incorporated into each week. The videos are available to you in The Locker Room University as a corresponding course to accompany the T.R.A.C.K. workbook. Full of inspiration and productivity hacks, the video modules will help you become more effective and educated throughout your 12-week T.R.A.C.K. experience.

ACTIVITY TRACKER

To know where you are going, you must know where you have been. Anything that is measured can be improved, so it is one of the most critical aspects of T.R.A.C.K. to document your activities and results on the provided activity tracker within each week. Experience has shown that real estate agents tend to resist tracking their numbers. Various reasons and excuses lead to this, but our belief system is numbers are the language of business. If you are not tracking your numbers and extracting the story that they are telling, then this means you are running your business on an emotional ebb and flow. Our studies show this is what will lead to missed goals, a victim mindset, and, ultimately, the overwhelming attrition rate in our industry. Numbers can expose so many things about the reality of what's happening in your business. If you do not make it a habit to document your activities and results, then you're merely guessing and will create fictional stories in your mind as to why you're not getting the results you desire.

We cannot emphasize enough to commit to the entire process, which includes tracking your progress during and beyond the completion of our T.R.A.C.K. program.

ACTIVITY TRACKER - DATES: _____

	MON	TUES	WED	THURS	FRI	SAT	SUN	ACTUAL	GOAL	TOTAL
ACTIVITIES										
Contacts Made										
Contacts Added to Database										
FSBO Contacts Made										
Expired Contacts Made										
Social Media Contacts Made										
# of Handwritten Notes										
# of Open Houses Held										
# of Doors Knocked										
# of Minutes Script Practicing										
BUSINESS										
Buyer Appointments Held										
Buyer Agency Agreements Signed										
Accepted Buyer Contracts Written										
New Listing Appointments Held										
New Listings Taken										
New Closings From Buyers										
New Closings From Sellers										
Total Closed Volume (Buyer + Seller)										

NOTES / AHA'S

HOW TO TACKLE EACH WEEK

GET YOUR WORKBOOK PAGES READY! THIS WORKBOOK AND THE VIDEO COURSES WORK HAND IN HAND.

USE THE WEEKLY PLANNER PAGES TO SCHEDULE YOUR WEEK AND MAKE SURE TO USE THE WEEKLY CHECKLIST SO YOU INCLUDE ALL T.R.A.C.K. ACTIVITIES.

USE THE WEEKLY ACTIVITY CHECKLIST TO MAKE SURE YOU COVER ALL VIDEOS, ACTIVITIES, AND TASKS.

GRAB THE ACTIVITY TRACKER AND RECORD YOUR PROGRESS AND SUCCESSES THROUGHOUT THE WEEK.

KNOCKOUT THE WEEKLY CHALLENGE!

FEELING NERVOUS?

KEEP IN MIND, SOME OF THE BEST HITTERS IN MAJOR LEAGUE BASEBALL HISTORY END UP IN THE HALL OF FAME BY SUCCEEDING 3 OUT OF 10 TIMES.

WHAT IS YOUR SCOREBOARD?
HOW ARE YOU GOING TO KEEP IT AS THE FOCAL POINT THAT DRIVES YOUR ACTIVITIES AND SKILL SET DEVELOPMENT?

You've got this.

FOUNDATION
WEEK 1

Week 1 is the start of our Foundation section and is all about clarity around your goals. You will be asked to complete the Agent Action Plan Series so you know what it is you're striving to achieve along with your plan of action to make it a reality. This powerful workbook will leave you with clarity, knowledge around your big why, and the measurable actions to focus on to produce the outcome you desire. It is time to apply your commitment to the process and consistency to the activities that it will take to achieve your goals!

LET'S GET STARTED | *How to access the video content each week:*

1. Go to LockerRoomUniversity.com where you first purchased or accessed Agent T.R.A.C.K.
2. Log into the account you created at the time of purchase or one you already have created
3. Click on Dashboard
4. Find the Agent T.R.A.C.K. Course and click "Start Course" (Search: TRACK)
4. Watch Welcome Video

Each week the videos and accompanying materials are set up in chapters. Watch the videos at the beginning of each week to get a firm grasp on the activities. We know it's tempting, but **DON'T SKIP AHEAD**. There's a method to this madness.

JOIN "THE LOCKER ROOM NATION" FACEBOOK GROUP

This community is all about support, sharing, and growth! A place to share your successes, tips, what's working in your business, favorite resources, and ask for advice. Join, and you'll also gain access to coaching from top Locker Room Coaches and a network of thousands of agents all across the Nation and access to The Locker Room Huddle.

WEEK 1 | ACTIVITIES: THE AGENT ACTION PLAN

WHERE	ACTIVITY	RESOURCE	WORKSHEETS	✓
Task	**UPDATE** Weekly Calendar	T.R.A.C.K. Workbook	PG 10-11	
Task	**WRITE** 10 Handwritten Notes	TLR Scripts Booklet	PG 12	
Task	**ADD** 30 People To Your Database	Activity Tracker	PG 12	
Task	**MAKE** a Minimum of 50 Contacts #TLRTenADay	Activity Tracker / TLR Scripts Booklet	PG 12	
Task	**SET** 2 New Appointments	Activity Tracker	PG 12	
Task	**SCRIPT / ROLE PLAY** at least 15 minutes per day	TLR Scripts Booklet		
Challenge	**COMPLETE THE WEEKLY CHALLENGE:** The Amazing Prospecting Race	T.R.A.C.K. Workbook	PG 25: The Amazing Prospecting Race Challenge	
Online	**LOG INTO** The Locker Room University Account	LockerRoomUniversity.com	Read Welcome to T.R.A.C.K.! It's time to get your jersey dirty!	
Online	**WATCH:** Let's Get Started! The Locker Room CEO, Jake Dixon	LockerRoomUniversity.com	Download & Print T.R.A.C.K. Workbook and Scripts Book	
Online	**WATCH:** Introduction to the Foundation Section (2m)	LockerRoomUniversity.com		
Online	**WATCH & COMPLETE:** Agent Action Plan: Financial Goals (26m)	LockerRoomUniversity.com	PG 13: Financial Goals	
Online	**WATCH & COMPLETE:** Agent Action Plan: Your Database Plan (9m)	LockerRoomUniversity.com	PG 14: Your Database Plan	
Online	**WATCH & COMPLETE:** Agent Action Plan: Behavior Based Lead Gen Strategy (12m)	LockerRoomUniversity.com	PG 15: Behavior Based Lead Gen Strategy	
Online	**WATCH & COMPLETE:** Core Relationships (10m)	LockerRoomUniversity.com	PG 16: Core Relationships	
Online	**WATCH & COMPLETE:** Agent Action Plan: Nurturing Your Database (10m)	LockerRoomUniversity.com	PG 17: Nurturing Your Database	
Online	**WATCH & COMPLETE:** Agent Action Plan: Expenses & Cost of Sales (9m)	LockerRoomUniversity.com	PG 18: Expenses & Cost of Sales	
Online	**WATCH & COMPLETE:** Agent Action Plan: The Vision of Your Business (6m)	LockerRoomUniversity.com	PG 19: The Vision of Your Business	
Online	**WATCH & COMPLETE:** Agent Action Plan: Your Simplified Business Plan (ROI) (12m)	LockerRoomUniversity.com	PG 20: Your Simplified Business Plan	
Online	**WATCH & COMPLETE:** Agent Action Plan: 5 Year Plan (10m)	LockerRoomUniversity.com	PG 21: 5 Year Plan	
Online	**WATCH & COMPLETE:** Agent Action Plan: Unique Value Proposition (10m)	LockerRoomUniversity.com	PG 22: Unique Value Proposition	
Online	**WATCH & COMPLETE:** Determining Your "BIG WHY" and Letters To Your Family (16m)	LockerRoomUniversity.com	PG 23: Determining Your "BIG WHY" / PG 24: Letters To Your Family	

WWW.TLRNATION.COM

WEEK 1 Calendar

MONDAY _____	TUESDAY _____	WEDNESDAY _____
PRIORITIES	**PRIORITIES**	**PRIORITIES**
1.	1.	1.
2.	2.	2.
3.	3.	3.
6:00AM	6:00AM	6:00AM
7:00AM	7:00AM	7:00AM
8:00AM	8:00AM	8:00AM
9:00AM	9:00AM	9:00AM
10:00AM	10:00AM	10:00AM
11:00AM	11:00AM	11:00AM
12:00AM	12:00AM	12:00AM
1:00PM	1:00PM	1:00PM
2:00PM	2:00PM	2:00PM
3:00PM	3:00PM	3:00PM
4:00PM	4:00PM	4:00PM
5:00PM	5:00PM	5:00PM
6:00PM	6:00PM	6:00PM
7:00PM	7:00PM	7:00PM
8:00PM	8:00PM	8:00PM

CALENDAR HOW TO:

1ST: Personal & Family Time
Date Night, Vacations, Birthdays, etc.

2ND: Events & Other Immovable Things
Lead Gen, Coaching Calls, Trainings, etc.

3RD: Predetermined Appointment Slots
Listing Appts, Showings, Open Houses etc.

4TH: Everything Else
TRACK Activities, Follow up, Transaction Work, Emails, etc.

CURRENT PENDINGS

SELLERS	NOTES / TO DO

BUYERS	NOTES / TO DO

THURSDAY _____	FRIDAY _____	SATURDAY _____
PRIORITIES	**PRIORITIES**	8:00AM
1.	1.	9:00AM
2.	2.	10:00AM
3.	3.	11:00AM
6:00AM	6:00AM	12:00AM
7:00AM	7:00AM	1:00PM
8:00AM	8:00AM	2:00PM
9:00AM	9:00AM	3:00PM
10:00AM	10:00AM	4:00PM
11:00AM	11:00AM	5:00PM
12:00AM	12:00AM	6:00PM
1:00PM	1:00PM	7:00PM
2:00PM	2:00PM	8:00PM
3:00PM	3:00PM	**SUNDAY** _____
4:00PM	4:00PM	8:00AM
5:00PM	5:00PM	9:00AM
6:00PM	6:00PM	10:00AM
7:00PM	7:00PM	11:00AM
8:00PM	8:00PM	12:00AM
MUST DO		1:00PM
		2:00PM
		3:00PM
		4:00PM
		5:00PM
		6:00PM
		7:00PM
		8:00PM

ACTIVITY TRACKER - DATES: _____

ACTIVITIES	MON	TUES	WED	THURS	FRI	SAT	SUN	ACTUAL	GOAL	TOTAL
Contacts Made										
Contacts Added to Database										
FSBO Contacts Made										
Expired Contacts Made										
Social Media Contacts Made										
# of Handwritten Notes										
# of Open Houses Held										
# of Doors Knocked										
# of Minutes Script Practicing										

BUSINESS	MON	TUES	WED	THURS	FRI	SAT	SUN	ACTUAL	GOAL	TOTAL
Buyer Appointments Held										
Buyer Agency Agreements Signed										
Accepted Buyer Contracts Written										
New Listing Appointments Held										
New Listings Taken										
New Closings From Buyers										
New Closings From Sellers										
Total Closed Volume (Buyer + Seller)										

NOTES / AHA'S

AGENT ACTION PLAN: FINANCIAL GOALS
How Much Money Do You Want To Net?

NET	A = How much do you want to Net in 1 year?	$
+ Cost of Sales	B = Brokerage Split/Royalty, Buyer's Agent Split, Transaction Coordinator	$
+ Expenses	C = Yearly Operating Expenses	$
+ Taxes	D = Example: 30% to taxes (A ÷ .70) - A	$
TOTAL GCI	E = A + B + C + D	$
Avg Sales Price	F = What is your projected average sales price?	$
Avg Commission	G = What is your average commission per deal?	$
Total Closed Units	H = E / G	
Total Closed Volume	I = H x F	$
% of Business	What % of your business will come from Listings vs. Buyers? *Recommended is 50% for individual agents.*	%
Listings Sold	J = H x % of Business from Listings	
Listings Taken	J / 75% Conversion of Listings Taken to Listings Sold. *Example: 12 Listings Sold / .75 = 16 Listings Taken to close 12 Listings*	
Listing Appts	Listings Taken divided by 50% Conversion of Listing Appointments to Listing Taken. Adjust accordingly for your percentage. *Example: 12 Listings Taken / .5 = 24 Listing Appointments needed to take 12 listings*	
% of Business	What % of your business will come from Listings vs. Buyers? *Recommended is 50% for individual agents.*	
Buyers Sold	Closed Units x % of Business from Buyers =	
Buyer Contracts Written	Closed Buyers divided by 75% Conversion of Buyer Contracts Written to Buyers Sold. Will 7.5 out of 10 buyer contracts written end up closing? *Example: 12 Buyers Sold / .75 = 16 Buyer Contracts Written to close 12 Buyer Side sales*	
Buyer Appts	Buyer Contracts Written divided by 50% Conversion of Buyer Appts to Buyer Contracts Written. Adjust accordingly for your percentage. *Example: 16 Buyer Contracts Written / .5 = 32 Buyer Appointments needed to write 16 Accepted Buyer Contracts*	
Appts per Week	Listing Appt + Buyer Appt = Annual Appointments Needed **Annual Appointments Needed divided by 48 work weeks =**	
Relationships/ Database	20:1 Ratio (5%) Return on Warm Database. Closed Unit Goal divided by .05 *Example: 24 Closed Units Goal / .05 = 480 Warm Database Names Needed*	
Marketing	50:1 Ratio (2%) Return on Cold Database. Closed Unit Goal divided by .02. *Example: 24 Closed Units Goal / .02 = 1,200 Cold Database Names Needed*	

AGENT ACTION PLAN: YOUR DATABASE PLAN
Growing a Relationship Based Business

DATABASE PLAN OPTIONS:

OPTION #1: WARM Database Only *(Someone who knows you as a real estate agent)*

OPTION #2: COLD Database Only *(Anyone you have not introduced yourself to as a real estate agent)*

OPTION #3: Combination of WARM & COLD Databases *(Recommended)*

MY DATABASE GAP ANALYSIS:

	ANSWER
A = What % of your business is going to come from your warm database?	%
B = What % of your business is going to come from your cold database?	%
C = How many closed units do I need from my warm database? A x Total Closed Units to Meet Goal (Line H on pg 14)	
D = How many closed units do I need from my cold database? B x Total Closed Units to Meet Goal (Line H on page 14)	
E = Goal number of warm database names I need C ÷ 5%	
F = Goal number of cold database names I need D ÷ 2%	

	WARM	COLD
Goal	E =	F =
- Actual Number In Your Database		
= # of Contacts I Need to Add		
÷ 6 = Database Additions Per Month		

One individual practicing sportsmanship is far better than 60 preaching it.

AGENT ACTION PLAN: BEHAVIOR BASED LEAD GENERATION STRATEGY
Play To Your Strengths To Generate Business

DOMINANCE		INFLUENCE	
Dominance Options For Prospecting	**Dominance Options For Marketing**	**Influence Options For Prospecting**	**Influence Options For Marketing**
x Cold Call: FSBO, Expired, Circle Prospecting x Door Knocking x Target Home Builders (On-site or Builder) x Business Owners (Allied Resources) x Sponsor Events x SOI x Agent to Agent Referrals x Core Advocates	x Branded Gear (Clothes, Badge, Car) x Referral Reward Program x Google Ads x Geographical Farming x Donating Publicly (w/ getting credit)	x Hosting "Lifestyle" Events (In home, etc.) x Networking Events x Client Appreciation Parties x Social Media (Private Messages, Posts, Live Videos) x Open Houses x SOI x Volunteering in Community x Agent to Agent Referrals x Core Advocates	x Client Referral Program x Advertising x Swag with Face & Branding x Car Wrap
STEADINESS		**COMPLIANCE**	
Steadiness Options For Prospecting	**Steadiness Options For Prospecting**	**Compliance Options For Prospecting**	**Compliance Options For Marketing**
x Home Buyer/Seller Seminars x Networking Events x Business Owners (Allied Resources) x Social Media Groups / Private Messages x New Home Builders x 1:1 Small Group Meetings (Lunch/Coffee) x Pop By Ideas x SOI x Handwritten Notes x Core Advocates x Community Events x Volunteering	x Branded Gear x Client Referral Program x Car Wrap Advertising	x SEO / Click Funnels x Social Media (Private Messages) x 1:1 Small Group Meetings (Lunch/Coffee) x Gather Cards From Tack Boards (Gyms, Coffee Shops) x SOI x Open Houses x Pop By Ideas x Handwritten Notes x Core Advocates x Community Events x Volunteering x Trade Show Booth	x Branded Gear / Swag x Online Testimonials with Stats x Direct Mailers x Geographical Farming x Online Leads x Car Wraps / Decals

AGENT ACTION PLAN: CORE RELATIONSHIPS
Real Estate Is A Relationship Based Business

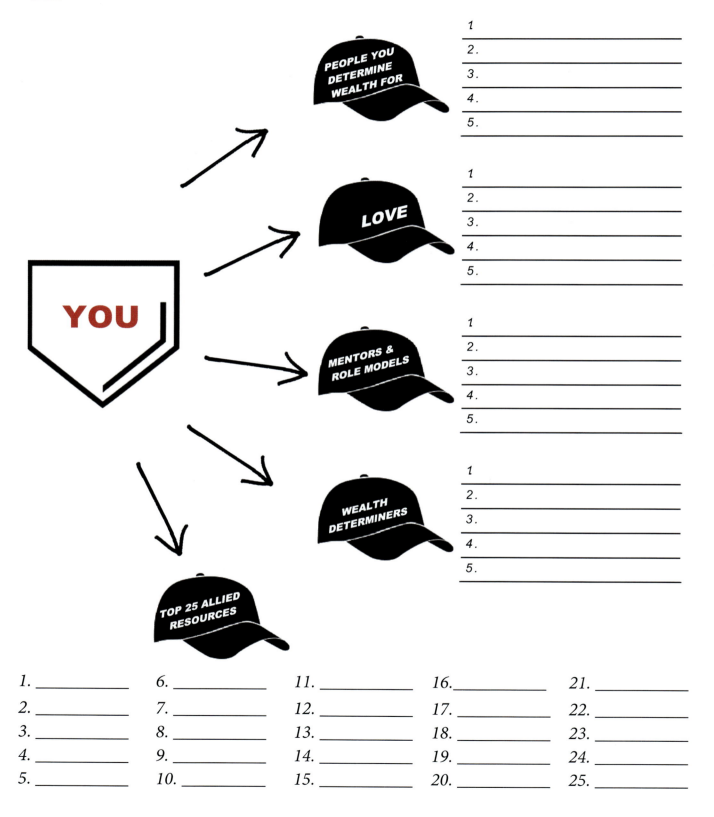

AGENT ACTION PLAN: NURTURING YOUR DATABASE
How To Market Yourself And Stay Top Of Mind

NAME OF CONTACT GROUP:	TYPE & NAME OF OUTREACH PLAN:	ALL EMAIL / ALL DIRECT / COMBO:
1.		
2.		
3.		
4.		
5.		
6.		
7.		
8.		
9.		
10.		
11.		
12.		
13.		
14.		
15.		

NAME OF CONTACT GROUP:

Group your contacts in a CRM or spreadsheet according to how you know them, such as their location, interests, Warm Database vs. Cold Database, how you met them, or any other classification that will help you target them specifically. The same person can be in more than one group – do not overthink it.

TYPE AND NAME OF OUTREACH PLAN:

Now that you have grouped your contacts appropriately, provide them relevant information as it pertains to their current situation or timeline. The type of outreach plan helps determine the type of information they will receive and the frequency at which they receive it. For example, you have a contact group of "buyer prospects that are looking to purchase in the next 30 days". An outreach plan for this contact group would be making sure they receive daily communication about available homes and loan information.

ALL EMAIL / ALL DIRECT / COMBO:

Many outreach plans give you the option to have the "touches" be all email form, so it's cost-sensitive, or all direct contact (mail, phone call, in-person), or a combination of both. Identify what specific plan you are selecting and the layers and methods of communication, whether direct or indirect.

AGENT ACTION PLAN: EXPENSES AND COST OF SALES
Determine Your Cash Flow Needs

CATEGORY	THIS YEAR'S BUDGET	THIS YEAR'S BUDGET % OF GCI
COSTS OF SALES (COS):		
1. Amount Paid into Company *(Company Split)*		
2. Other COS *(Buyer's Agent, Transaction Coordinator, etc.)*		
Total Cost of Sales (COS):		

OPERATING EXPENSES:		
1. Salaries		
2. Lead Generation		
3. Marketing		
4. Office Bill/Rent		
5. Supplies/Equipment/Signs/Cards		
6. Education & Training		
7. MLS & Board Dues		
8. Meals & Entertainment		
9. Other:		
10. Other:		
Total Operating Expenses:		

TOTAL EXPENSES: (COS + Operating Expenses)		

Take home the win!

AGENT ACTION PLAN: THE VISION OF YOUR BUSINESS
Determine How You Want Your Business To Look In 12 Months

1. Draw the Organizational Structure that represents where your business will be in 12 months.

2. Write down your action plan for making this happen. Include what recruiting sources you will use and what compensation options you will offer.

AGENT ACTION PLAN: YOUR SIMPLIFIED BUSINESS PLAN (ROI)
Determine Your Main Objective And How To Achieve It

WHAT IS YOUR YEARLY GOAL?

THE 3 PILLARS TO SUCCESS

RELATIONSHIPS Mind Share for NURTURE Business	**OPPORTUNITY** Low Hanging Fruit for NOW Business	**INVESTMENT** Money/Time Spent for NEW Business

5 KEY ACTION ITEMS

1. Phone/Text:	1.	1.
2. Email:	2.	2.
3. Face-to-Face:	3.	3.
4. Direct Mail:	4.	4.
5. Social Media Messaging:	5.	5.

AGENT ACTION PLAN: 5 YEAR PLAN
It's Not About the Destination, It's About the Journey

5 YEARS FROM NOW: _____
(CURRENT YEAR + 5)

RELATIONSHIPS	BUSINESS
SPIRITUAL/HEALTH	**FINANCIAL**
EXPERIENCES	**INTELLECTUAL**
HAPPINESS	**CONTRIBUTION**

AGENT ACTION PLAN: UNIQUE VALUE PROPOSITION
Understand Who You Are And What Your Business Is About

MISSION STATEMENT: What is your purpose? Why are you in business?

CORE VALUES: What is important to you? What do you value? What is the "why" behind your business? What are your priorities?

BELIEF SYSTEM: What are the rules and guidelines you will follow?

AGENT ACTION PLAN: DETERMINING YOUR "BIG WHY"
How Is Real Estate Going to Effect Your Life?

If your WHY is big enough, then the HOW does not matter.
Your WHY should make you cry. Ask yourself, why is that my WHY? Dig deeper.

What stirs your soul? What makes your heart sing?
_____
_____

What is/was your driving motivation - the why, or goal, for a career in real estate?
_____
_____

What will achieving your goal mean for you?
_____
_____

In what ways will your life change?
_____
_____

What doors will open for you?
_____
_____

MY BIG WHY IS:
_____
_____

What could get in the way of achieving your Big Why?
_____
_____

How can you prevent that?
_____
_____

AGENT ACTION PLAN: LETTERS TO YOUR FAMILY
Messages For Your Family

MISSION: Use the space below to write two letters as if you were one year into the future. The first letter should describe in specific detail the feeling, emotion, and the way life looks when you accomplish your goals. The second letter should explain in specific detail the feeling, emotion, and the way life looks if you do not achieve your goals. Take your time, be precise, and allow yourself to go to that place to feel what it would be like in both scenarios.

SUCCESS LETTER:

APOLOGY LETTER:

WEEKLY CHALLENGE: THE AMAZING PROSPECTING RACE

The Amazing Prospecting Race is a fun way to jump start your T.R.A.C.K. journey by getting yourself into massive action to help achieve your Week 1 objectives. It will get you outside of your comfort zone by lead generating and creating new relationships so you can build a strong business for years to come. The only question is, are you ready to get your jersey dirty? Real estate is a contact sport, so it is time to make some meaningful contacts!

INSTRUCTIONS: Complete as many activities as you can.
Enter an "x" in the corresponding column once you complete the activity.

POINTS:
- x 1 point = Completing the activity
- x 1 point = Taking a photo of the activity and post to "The Locker Room Nation" Facebook group
- x 1 point = Getting the person's contact information

ACTIVITIES	DONE	INFO	SELFIE
Go into a donut shop and give a stranger your card			
Talk to a stranger in a department store or the mall and give them your card			
Talk to a stranger at a bus stop and give them your card			
Introduce yourself to someone from a local Mortgage Company and exchange business cards			
Talk to 2 or more people standing together and give them your card			
Shake hands with a For Sale By Owner and give them your card			
Shake hands with a Renter and give them your card – EXTRA POINT if they agree to a buyer consultation			
Stop by at a new construction sales office and give the on-site agent your card			
Give your card to someone walking a dog & ask if they know anyone in the area looking to buy/sell			
Talk to a stranger in the diaper isle of Walmart or Target and give them your card			
Call a For Sale By Owner and EXTRA POINT if they agree to meet with you for a listing consultation			
Go into a Barber Shop or Hair Salon and give a stranger getting a haircut your card			
Give a waiter or waitress at a restaurant your card			
Go up to a family sitting at a restaurant and give them your card			
Go to Lowe's or Home Depot and give your card to the person who mixes paint			
Attend a networking event and exchange 5 business cards with local business owners			
Door knock an expired listing and give them your card EXTRA POINT if they agree to meet with you			
Shake hands with a Manager of a retirement home and give them your card			
Visit a Spa or Medical Center and give the person working the front desk your card			
Visit a Manager of any Hotel and give them your card			
Stop by a home of someone in your database and ask for a referral			
Visit a Doctor's office and give them your card			
Shake hands with a clerk of any hardware store and give them your card			
Give the gas station attendant your card			
Visit a car dealership and give a salesperson your card			
Shake hands with a police officer and give them your card			
Shake hands with a fire fighter and give them your card			
Make 10 Calls to Friends in your Database and ask for referral			
Stop in bridal store and give business card to consultant			
Door knock 10 homes in the neighborhood you live in and ask for referrals			
Write 10 hand written follow up notes and mail / personally deliver to your warm database			
Introduce yourself to a Financial Planner or Insurance Agent and give them your business card			
Visit a fitness center and introduce yourself to Director and give them your business card			
Sub Total:			
TOTAL			

WWW.TLRNATION.COM

DO IT FOR YOU!

TO ACCOMPLISH GREAT THINGS, WE MUST NOT ONLY ACT, BUT ALSO DREAM, NOT ONLY PLAN, BUT ALSO BELIEVE.

DON'T WAIT FOR AN OPPORTUNITY. CREATE IT.

Play like a champ!

FOUNDATION
WEEK 2

Week 2 focuses on prioritizing your time and creating a calendar that reflects your goals. You will be challenged to look differently at how you are utilizing your time and complete exercises that align with your priorities to help reduce your stress and allow you to operate more effectively and efficiently. It's not about selling real estate, it's about following a schedule!

WEEK 2 | ACTIVITIES: TIME MANAGEMENT

WHERE	ACTIVITY	RESOURCE	WORKSHEETS	✓
Task	**INTERVIEW** 1 Top Agent	Appendix	PG 127: Interview Questions	
Task	**HOLD 2** Breakthrough Open Houses	Appendix	PG 124 - 126: OH Strategies	
Task	**UPDATE** Weekly Calendar	T.R.A.C.K. Workbook	PG 30 - 31	
Task	**MAKE** a Minimum of 50 Contacts #TLRTenADay	Activity Tracker TLR Scripts Booklet	PG 29	
Task	**WRITE 10** Handwritten Notes	Activity Tracker TLR Scripts Booklet	PG 29	
Task	**ADD 30** People to Database	Activity Tracker	PG 29	
Task	**SCRIPT/ROLE PLAY** At Least 15 Minutes Per Day	Activity Tracker	PG 29	
Online	**WATCH:** Mindset Minute: Time Management (2m)	LockerRoomUniversity.com		
Online	**WATCH:** Time Management: Introduction (2m)	LockerRoomUniversity.com		
Online	**WATCH:** Time Management: What's the Real Issue (11m)	LockerRoomUniversity.com		
Online	**WATCH:** Time Management: 6 Human Needs Overview (3m)	LockerRoomUniversity.com	PG 32	
Online	**WATCH:** Time Management: (18m) 6 Human Needs: Connection - Contribution	LockerRoomUniversity.com	PG 33	
Online	**WATCH:** Time Management: 6 Human Needs Discovery Exercise (17m)	LockerRoomUniversity.com	PG 33 - 34	
Online	**WATCH:** Time Management: (10m) Examine Reality - An Agent's Task List	LockerRoomUniversity.com	Download: Agent Task List	
Online	**WATCH:** Time Management: 4 Quadrants for Prioritization (6m)	LockerRoomUniversity.com	PG 35	
Online	**WATCH:** Time Management: The 80/20 Principle - A Realtor's 20% (9m)	LockerRoomUniversity.com	PG 36	
Online	**WATCH:** Time Management: What Is Your Time Worth (12m)	LockerRoomUniversity.com	Download: Dollar Per Hour Calculator	
Online	**WATCH:** Time Management: The Perfect Day (6m)	LockerRoomUniversity.com	PG 37 - 38	
Online	**WATCH:** Time Management: (12m) System For Scheduling Your Priorities	LockerRoomUniversity.com		
Online	**WATCH:** Time Management: Wrap Up (3m)			
Online	**WATCH & COMPLETE:** How To Use The Future Business Pipeline Tool (9m)	LockerRoomUniversity.com	Download: The Future Business Pipeline	
Challenge	**COMPLETE THE WEEKLY CHALLENGE:** The Perfect Week Exercise	T.R.A.C.K. Workbook	PG 39	

ACTIVITY TRACKER - DATES: _____

	MON	TUES	WED	THURS	FRI	SAT	SUN	ACTUAL	GOAL	TOTAL
ACTIVITIES										
Contacts Made										
Contacts Added to Database										
FSBO Contacts Made										
Expired Contacts Made										
Social Media Contacts Made										
# of Handwritten Notes										
# of Open Houses Held										
# of Doors Knocked										
# of Minutes Script Practicing										
BUSINESS										
Buyer Appointments Held										
Buyer Agency Agreements Signed										
Accepted Buyer Contracts Written										
New Listing Appointments Held										
New Listings Taken										
New Closings From Buyers										
New Closings From Sellers										
Total Closed Volume (Buyer + Seller)										

NOTES / AHA'S

WEEK 2 Calendar

MONDAY _____	TUESDAY _____	WEDNESDAY _____
PRIORITIES	**PRIORITIES**	**PRIORITIES**
1.	1.	1.
2.	2.	2.
3.	3.	3.
6:00AM	6:00AM	6:00AM
7:00AM	7:00AM	7:00AM
8:00AM	8:00AM	8:00AM
9:00AM	9:00AM	9:00AM
10:00AM	10:00AM	10:00AM
11:00AM	11:00AM	11:00AM
12:00AM	12:00AM	12:00AM
1:00PM	1:00PM	1:00PM
2:00PM	2:00PM	2:00PM
3:00PM	3:00PM	3:00PM
4:00PM	4:00PM	4:00PM
5:00PM	5:00PM	5:00PM
6:00PM	6:00PM	6:00PM
7:00PM	7:00PM	7:00PM
8:00PM	8:00PM	8:00PM

CALENDAR HOW TO:

1ST: Personal & Family Time
Date Night, Vacations, Birthdays, etc.

2ND: Events & Other Immovable Things
Lead Gen, Coaching Calls, Trainings, etc.

3RD: Predetermined Appointment Slots
Listing Appts, Showings, Open Houses etc.

4TH: Everything Else
TRACK Activities, Follow up, Transaction Work, Emails, etc.

CURRENT PENDINGS

SELLERS	NOTES / TO DO

BUYERS	NOTES / TO DO

THURSDAY _____	FRIDAY _____	SATURDAY _____
PRIORITIES	**PRIORITIES**	8:00AM
1.	1.	9:00AM
2.	2.	10:00AM
3.	3.	11:00AM
6:00AM	6:00AM	12:00AM
7:00AM	7:00AM	1:00PM
8:00AM	8:00AM	2:00PM
9:00AM	9:00AM	3:00PM
10:00AM	10:00AM	4:00PM
11:00AM	11:00AM	5:00PM
12:00AM	12:00AM	6:00PM
1:00PM	1:00PM	7:00PM
2:00PM	2:00PM	8:00PM
3:00PM	3:00PM	**SUNDAY** _____
4:00PM	4:00PM	8:00AM
5:00PM	5:00PM	9:00AM
6:00PM	6:00PM	10:00AM
7:00PM	7:00PM	11:00AM
8:00PM	8:00PM	12:00AM
MUST DO		1:00PM
		2:00PM
		3:00PM
		4:00PM
		5:00PM
		6:00PM
		7:00PM
		8:00PM

WWW.TLRNATION.COM

TIME MANAGEMENT: STOP MAKING EXCUSES

The Six Human Needs Overview | *There is not enough time in the day to do everything, but there is enough time in the day to do the most important things.*

The Four Needs of The Personality

The Two Needs of The Spirit

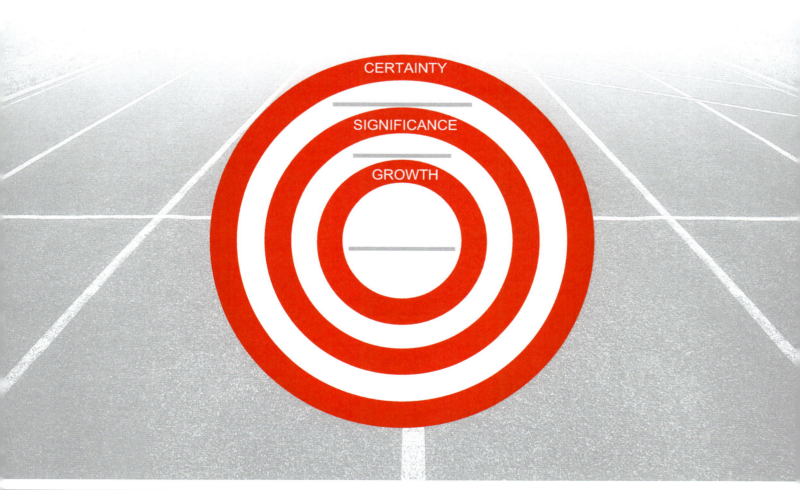

TIME MANAGEMENT: STOP MAKING EXCUSES
Discovery Exercise: The Six Human Needs

CONNECTION:

SIGNIFICANCE:

CERTAINTY:

VARIETY:

GROWTH:

CONTRIBUTION:

What are the ways you get certainty in your life? *Identify which ways are positive and/or negative.*

_____
_____
_____
_____

What are the ways you get variety in your life? *Identify which ways are positive and/or negative.*

_____
_____
_____
_____

What are the ways you get significance in your life? *Identify which ways are positive and/or negative.*

_____
_____
_____
_____

Of the (6) Human Needs, which two have you been valuing the most? *Rank them in order.*

What are the consequences of valuing those needs in that order?

What do your top (2) needs need to be now for your life to transform?

If you made that change, what would transform in your life?

TIME MANAGEMENT: STOP MAKING EXCUSES
The 4 Quadrants for Prioritization

HIGH   **URGENCY**   **LOW**

IMPORTANCE

1 Urgent & Important	**2** Important & NOT Urgent
4 Urgent & NOT Important	**3** NOT Urgent & NOT Important

LOW

Notes:

TIME MANAGEMENT: STOP MAKING EXCUSES
The Pareto Law (The 80/20 Principle)

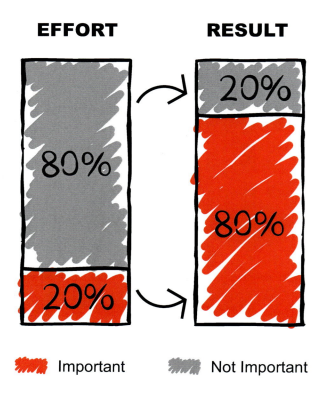

A REALTOR'S 20%:

1.
2.
3.
4.
5.

UTILIZE YOUR PLANNER PAGES

Every section of TRACK is complete with a weekly planner page so you can map out when you'll accomplish all of the activities for the week. We have provided you with a proven "how to" system for completing your planner each week:

1ST: Personal & Family Time, Date Night, Vacations, Birthdays, Family Time, Pick Up Kids From School, etc.

2ND: Events & Other Immovable Items Lead Generation, Coaching Calls, Training Events, Sales Meetings, etc.

3RD: Predetermined Appointment Slots, Listing Appts., Buyer Consultations, Showings, Open Houses, etc.

4TH: Everything Else, Follow Up, Transaction Work, TRACK Activities, Emails, etc.

It is not only possible to accomplish more by doing less, it is mandatory.

FULL TIME AGENT DAILY SCHEDULE

8:00am – 8:30am

LEAD GENERATION PREP

Contacts, scripts & materials ready. Role-play conducted. Distractions eliminated.

8:30am - 11:00am

LEAD GENERATION

Contacts made to Sphere of Influence, Geographic Farms, Expired Listings, FSBO, Just Listed/Just Sold or other purposeful business generating activities.

11:00am – NOON

BUSINESS SERVICING

Return emails, texts & calls received during lead conversion time. Also service listings, buyers & pending transactions.

Noon - 1:00pm

LUNCH

This is your time so take a break from work & eat with a friend, spouse or co-worker.

1:00pm - 2:00pm

LEAD GENERATION

Contacts made to Sphere of Influence, Geographic Farms, Expired Listings, FSBO, Just Listed/Just Sold or other purposeful business generating activities.

2:00pm – 3:00pm

BUSINESS SERVICING

Return emails, texts & calls received during lead conversion time. Also service listings, buyers & pending transactions.

3:00pm – 6:00pm

LISTING APPTS & SHOWINGS

All listing appointments & property showings should be scheduled during this time to allow lead generation & business servicing activities to be conducted prior.

6:00pm – SLEEP

PERSONAL/FAMILY TIME

Phone is shut down no later than 6:30pm each night. If listing & showing appointments are completed prior to 6:00pm, then get home early.

WWW.TLRNATION.COM

DUAL CAREER AGENT
DAILY SCHEDULE

ASSUMING A 9-5 WORKDAY

7:00am – 7:30am

SCRIPT/ROLE PLAY
Have a partner to practice with via phone call.

8:00am – 8:45am
on way to work

LEAD GENERATION
Contacts made to Sphere of Influence, Geographic Farms, Expired Listings, FSBO, Just Listed/Just Sold or other purposeful business generating activities.

12:15pm – 12:45pm
lunch break

BUSINESS SERVICING
Return emails, texts & calls received during lead conversion time. Also service listings, buyers & pending transactions.

6:00pm - 6:30pm
after dinner

LEAD GENERATION PREP
Contacts, scripts & materials ready. Role-play conducted. Distractions eliminated.

6:30pm - 8:30pm

LEAD GENERATION
Contacts made to Sphere of Influence, Geographic Farms, Expired Listings, FSBO, Just Listed/Just Sold or other purposeful business generating activities.

LISTING APPTS & SHOWINGS
All listing appointments & property showings should be scheduled during this time to allow lead generation & business servicing activities to be conducted prior.

8:30pm - 9:30pm

BUSINESS SERVICING
Return emails, texts & calls received during lead conversion time. Also service listings, buyers & pending transactions.

9:30pm - 10:00pm

LEAD GENERATION PREP
Contacts, scripts & materials ready. Role-play conducted. Distractions eliminated.

WEEKLY CHALLENGE: "The Perfect Week" Exercise
By making all the pieces fit together, you can have a productive and fulfilling week.

DIRECTIONS: What does your ideal week look like if you stuck to a perfect time-blocked schedule? Use the form below to structure your perfect week. Does it reflect your goals and priorities? Now let's get to work so this becomes your reality! Ready, Set, Go!

	MONDAY	TUESDAY	WEDNESDAY	THURSDAY	FRIDAY	SATURDAY	SUNDAY
7:00 AM							
8:00 AM							
9:00 AM							
10:00 AM							
11:00 AM							
12:00 PM							
1:00 PM							
2:00 PM							
3:00 PM							
4:00 PM							
5:00 PM							
6:00 PM							
7:00 PM							
8:00 PM							

DEDICATION + MOTIVATION = SUCCESS

IN THE END, YOU WILL ONLY REGRET THE CHANCES YOU DIDN'T TAKE.

Keep moving forward!

FOUNDATION
WEEK 3

Week 3 is lighter on the educational side now that you have your calendar and business plan in place. This is your chance to make sure your activities are happening consistently. From here, in week 3 we will dial in your focus by challenging you to consider who your Top 50 Core Advocates are and how you can earn their referrals.

WEEK 3 | ACTIVITIES: CORE ADVOCATES

WHERE	ACTIVITY	RESOURCE	WORKSHEETS	✓
Task	**INTERVIEW** 1 Top Agent	Appendix	PG 127: Interview Questions	
Task	**COFFEE OR LUNCH** with at least 2 Core Advocates from your list	Weekly Planner TLR Scripts Simplified Booklet	PG 44 - 45	
Task	**UPDATE** Weekly Calendar	T.R.A.C.K. Workbook	PG 44 - 45	
Task	**MAKE** a Minimum of 50 Contacts #TLRTenADay	Activity Tracker TLR Scripts Simplified Booklet	PG 43	
Task	**WRITE 10** Handwritten Notes	Activity Tracker TLR Scripts Simplified Booklet	PG 43	
Task	**ADD 30** people to Database	Activity Tracker	PG 43	
Task	**SET 2** new appointments	Activity Tracker	PG 43	
Task	**SHOOT 1** Facebook Live / Instagram video #TLRNation			
Task	**SCRIPT / ROLE PLAY** at least 15 minutes per day	Activity Tracker TLR Scripts Simplified Booklet	PG 44	
Challenge	**HOLD 2** Breakthrough Open Houses	Appendix	PG 124 - 126: TLR Open House Strategies	
Online	**WATCH:** Mindset Minute - Focus On Relationships (3m)	LockerRoomUniversity.com		
Online	**WATCH:** Top 50 Core Advocates: Why it's Important (11m)	LockerRoomUniversity.com		
Online	**WATCH & COMPLETE:** Create A List of Your Top 50 Core Advocates: Identifying Who They Are (3m)	LockerRoomUniversity.com	PG 46: Create A List of Your Top 50 Core Advocates: Identifying Who They Are	
Online	**VISIT** The Facebook Group & interact with our community	facebook.com/groups/LockerRoomNation		
Task	**COMPLETE** Foundation Section Goal Assessment	T.R.A.C.K. Workbook	PG 47	

ACTIVITY TRACKER - DATES:

	MON	TUES	WED	THURS	FRI	SAT	SUN	ACTUAL	GOAL	TOTAL
ACTIVITIES										
Contacts Made										
Contacts Added to Database										
FSBO Contacts Made										
Expired Contacts Made										
Social Media Contacts Made										
# of Handwritten Notes										
# of Open Houses Held										
# of Doors Knocked										
# of Minutes Script Practicing										
BUSINESS										
Buyer Appointments Held										
Buyer Agency Agreements Signed										
Accepted Buyer Contracts Written										
New Listing Appointments Held										
New Listings Taken										
New Closings From Buyers										
New Closings From Sellers										
Total Closed Volume (Buyer + Seller)										

NOTES / AHA'S

WEEK 3 Calendar

MONDAY _____	TUESDAY _____	WEDNESDAY _____
PRIORITIES	**PRIORITIES**	**PRIORITIES**
1.	1.	1.
2.	2.	2.
3.	3.	3.
6:00AM	6:00AM	6:00AM
7:00AM	7:00AM	7:00AM
8:00AM	8:00AM	8:00AM
9:00AM	9:00AM	9:00AM
10:00AM	10:00AM	10:00AM
11:00AM	11:00AM	11:00AM
12:00AM	12:00AM	12:00AM
1:00PM	1:00PM	1:00PM
2:00PM	2:00PM	2:00PM
3:00PM	3:00PM	3:00PM
4:00PM	4:00PM	4:00PM
5:00PM	5:00PM	5:00PM
6:00PM	6:00PM	6:00PM
7:00PM	7:00PM	7:00PM
8:00PM	8:00PM	8:00PM

CALENDAR HOW TO:

1ST: Personal & Family Time
Date Night, Vacations, Birthdays, etc.

2ND: Events & Other Immovable Things
Lead Gen, Coaching Calls, Trainings, etc.

3RD: Predetermined Appointment Slots
Listing Appts, Showings, Open Houses etc.

4TH: Everything Else
TRACK Activities, Follow up, Transaction Work, Emails, etc.

CURRENT PENDINGS

SELLERS	NOTES / TO DO

BUYERS	NOTES / TO DO

THURSDAY _____	FRIDAY _____	SATURDAY _____
PRIORITIES	**PRIORITIES**	8:00AM
1.	1.	9:00AM
2.	2.	10:00AM
3.	3.	11:00AM
6:00AM	6:00AM	12:00AM
7:00AM	7:00AM	1:00PM
8:00AM	8:00AM	2:00PM
9:00AM	9:00AM	3:00PM
10:00AM	10:00AM	4:00PM
11:00AM	11:00AM	5:00PM
12:00AM	12:00AM	6:00PM
1:00PM	1:00PM	7:00PM
2:00PM	2:00PM	8:00PM
3:00PM	3:00PM	**SUNDAY _____**
4:00PM	4:00PM	8:00AM
5:00PM	5:00PM	9:00AM
6:00PM	6:00PM	10:00AM
7:00PM	7:00PM	11:00AM
8:00PM	8:00PM	12:00AM

MUST DO		
		1:00PM
		2:00PM
		3:00PM
		4:00PM
		5:00PM
		6:00PM
		7:00PM
		8:00PM

CREATE A LIST OF YOUR TOP 50 CORE ADVOCATES
Identifying Who They Are

List your 50 Core Advocates. These are people in your database that, when they think of real estate, they think of you. They're willing to send you referrals on a regular to semi-regular basis actively. These are ideally well connected and influential people, such as vendor partners, close friends and family, influencers in the community, and previous clients.

1	26
2	27
3	28
4	29
5	30
6	31
7	32
8	33
9	34
10	35
11	36
12	37
13	38
14	39
15	40
16	41
17	42
18	43
19	44
20	45
21	46
22	47
23	48
24	49
25	50

CONGRATS! YOU FINISHED THE FOUNDATION SECTION OF T.R.A.C.K.!
FOUNDATION SECTION GOAL ASSESSMENT (WEEKS 1- 3)

The goal for the end of the Foundation section was to establish clarity around your goals, establish the activities it is going to take to achieve those goals and know how to protect your time so your calendar reflects your goals.

DONE	ACTIVITY
	Agent Action Plan Completed & Goals Set
	The Amazing Prospecting Race – Achieved at least 40 points
	150 Contacts Made
	90 Contacts Added to Database
	4 Appointments Set/Held
	4 Open Houses Held
	Perfect Week Implemented
	30 Handwritten Notes
	2 Coffee / Lunch Dates with Core Advocates or Preferred Vendors
	2 Top Agents Interviewed
	Establish Activity Tracking Habit
	Top 50 Core Advocates Identified

REFLECT AND WRITE YOUR AHA'S FROM THE FOUNDATION SECTION (WEEKS 1-3):

SUCCESS IS A CHOICE

Life is better with goals.

SKILLS
WEEK 4

"List to Last" is an old adage regarding what it takes to be successful in real estate. Week 4 is all about developing your skill set around taking more listings. We will dive into items such as For Sale by Owners, Expired Listings, and the art of perfecting your listing presentation. This is a powerful session so get ready to dive in and take more listings!

WEEK 4 | ACTIVITIES: LISTINGS AND SELLERS

WHERE	ACTIVITY	RESOURCE	WORKSHEETS	✓
Task	**SET 2 NEW APPTS** With a FSBO and/or Expired	TLR Scripts Booklet	PG 51	
Task	**HOLD 2** Breakthrough Open Houses	Appendix	PG 124 - 126: Breakthrough Open House Strategies	
Task	**COFFEE OR LUNCH** with at least 2 Core Advocates from your list	Weekly Planner TLR Scripts Booklet		
Task	**UPDATE** Weekly Calendar	T.R.A.C.K. Workbook	PG 52-53	
Task	**MAKE** a minimum of 50 Contacts #TLRTenADay	Activity Tracker TLR Scripts Simplified Booklet	PG 51	
Task	**WRITE 10** handwritten notes	Activity Tracker TLR Scripts Booklet	PG 51	
Task	**ADD 25** people to Database	Activity Tracker	PG 51	
Task	**SHOOT 1** Facebook Live / Instagram video #TLRNation			
Task	**SCRIPT / ROLE PLAY** at least 15 minutes per day	TLR Scripts Booklet	PG 51	
Online	**WATCH:** Introduction to the Skills Section (1m)	LockerRoomUniversity.com		
Online	**WATCH:** Mindset Minute: Ask for the Business (2m)	LockerRoomUniversity.com		
Online	**WATCH & COMPLETE:** Working with For Sale By Owners (19m)	LockerRoomUniversity.com	PG 54: FSBO Math	
Online	**WATCH & COMPLETE:** (20m) Working with Expired Listings	LockerRoomUniversity.com	PG 55: Working With Expired Listings	
Online	**WATCH:** Mastering Your Listing Presentation: Best Practices to Lead Generate For Listings (5m)	LockerRoomUniversity.com	PG 55: Lead Generation For Listings	
Online	**WATCH & COMPLETE:** Mastering Your Listing Presentation: Preparing for a Listing Appointment - The Essentials (6m)	LockerRoomUniversity.com	PG 56: Preparing for Your Listing Appointment	
Online	**WATCH:** (34m) Mastering Your Listing Presentation: The Listing Presentation Role Play	LockerRoomUniversity.com		
Task	**CREATE/REFINE/PREPARE** Your Listing Consultation	Listing Appointment Prep Checklist Appendix: Seller Lead Sheet	Download: Customizable Listing Presentation PPT	
Challenge	**PRACTICE/ROLE PLAY** A Listing Presentation with a Top Producer or Coach in the office	TLR Scripts Booklet		

ACTIVITY TRACKER - DATES: ____

	MON	TUES	WED	THURS	FRI	SAT	SUN	ACTUAL	GOAL	TOTAL
ACTIVITIES										
Contacts Made										
Contacts Added to Database										
FSBO Contacts Made										
Expired Contacts Made										
Social Media Contacts Made										
# of Handwritten Notes										
# of Open Houses Held										
# of Doors Knocked										
# of Minutes Script Practicing										
BUSINESS										
Buyer Appointments Held										
Buyer Agency Agreements Signed										
Accepted Buyer Contracts Written										
New Listing Appointments Held										
New Listings Taken										
New Closings From Buyers										
New Closings From Sellers										
Total Closed Volume (Buyer + Seller)										

NOTES / AHA'S

WEEK 4 Calendar

MONDAY _____	TUESDAY _____	WEDNESDAY _____
PRIORITIES	**PRIORITIES**	**PRIORITIES**
1.	1.	1.
2.	2.	2.
3.	3.	3.
6:00AM	6:00AM	6:00AM
7:00AM	7:00AM	7:00AM
8:00AM	8:00AM	8:00AM
9:00AM	9:00AM	9:00AM
10:00AM	10:00AM	10:00AM
11:00AM	11:00AM	11:00AM
12:00AM	12:00AM	12:00AM
1:00PM	1:00PM	1:00PM
2:00PM	2:00PM	2:00PM
3:00PM	3:00PM	3:00PM
4:00PM	4:00PM	4:00PM
5:00PM	5:00PM	5:00PM
6:00PM	6:00PM	6:00PM
7:00PM	7:00PM	7:00PM
8:00PM	8:00PM	8:00PM

CALENDAR HOW TO:

1ST: Personal & Family Time
Date Night, Vacations, Birthdays, etc.

2ND: Events & Other Immovable Things
Lead Gen, Coaching Calls, Trainings, etc.

3RD: Predetermined Appointment Slots
Listing Appts, Showings, Open Houses etc.

4TH: Everything Else
TRACK Activities, Follow up, Transaction Work, Emails, etc.

CURRENT PENDINGS

SELLERS	NOTES / TO DO

BUYERS	NOTES / TO DO

THURSDAY	FRIDAY	SATURDAY
PRIORITIES	**PRIORITIES**	8:00AM
1.	1.	9:00AM
2.	2.	10:00AM
3.	3.	11:00AM
6:00AM	6:00AM	12:00AM
7:00AM	7:00AM	1:00PM
8:00AM	8:00AM	2:00PM
9:00AM	9:00AM	3:00PM
10:00AM	10:00AM	4:00PM
11:00AM	11:00AM	5:00PM
12:00AM	12:00AM	6:00PM
1:00PM	1:00PM	7:00PM
2:00PM	2:00PM	8:00PM

SUNDAY
8:00AM
9:00AM
10:00AM
11:00AM
12:00AM
1:00PM
2:00PM
3:00PM
4:00PM
5:00PM
6:00PM
7:00PM
8:00PM

(Thursday/Friday continued: 3:00PM, 4:00PM, 5:00PM, 6:00PM, 7:00PM, 8:00PM)

MUST DO

WWW.TLRNATION.COM

FOR SALE BY OWNERS & EXPIRED LISTINGS
FSBO MATH

FOR SALE BY OWNER LISTING

List Price: $100,000

List to Sale Price Ratio: _____

Potential Net: _____

AGENT LISTING

List Price: $100,000

List to Sale Price Ratio: _____

6% Commission: _____

Potential Net: _____

Learning what the seller's _____ is what matters most.

3 QUESTIONS TO ASK TO DISCOVER A SELLER'S MOTIVATION:

1. _____
2. _____
3. _____

THE STEPS TO CONVERTING A FOR SALE BY OWNER:

Week 1. Preview the home.

Week 2. Prepare & Deliver: _____

Week 3. Prepare & Deliver: _____

Week 4. Prepare & Deliver: _____

Week 5. Prepare & Deliver: _____

Week 6. Prepare & Deliver: _____

Week 7. Prepare & Deliver: _____

Week 8. Prepare & Deliver: _____

FOR SALE BY OWNERS & EXPIRED LISTINGS
Working With Expired Listings

3 REASONS A HOME DOESN'T SELL:

1. _____
2. _____
3. _____

THE SECRET: When a home doesn't sell, it is always because of the _____.

TO GAIN THE ADVANTAGE WITH AN EXPIRED LISTING:

1. _____
2. _____
3. _____
4. _____

MASTERING YOUR LISTING PRESENTATION
Best Practices to Lead Generate For Listings

LEAD GENERATING FOR LISTINGS

When it comes to lead generation for listings, find what you are good at, passionate about and keep doing that.

1. _____ & _____
2. _____
3. _____
4. _____

When it comes to lead generating, _____ wins.

PREPARING FOR YOUR LISTING APPOINTMENT
Know Your Market and Be the Expert

1 - SEARCH YOUR LOCAL MLS 6 MONTHS BACK FOR:

1. Average _____
2. _____ to _____ Ratio
3. Number of homes _____
4. Number of homes _____

2 - PRICING: Always compare _____ to _____ .

3 - LISTING PRESENTATION OUTLINE:

1. _____
2. _____
3. _____

IDEAS OF THINGS TO INCLUDE IN YOUR LISTING PACKET:

- ✗ Total Market Overview (Current Market Statistics)
- ✗ Full CMA
- ✗ Estimate of Proceeds (Work with local title company on obtaining or creating a calculation)
- ✗ Marketing Materials/Sample Flyers
- ✗ Professional Photographer Information
- ✗ Stager Information
- ✗ Marketing Plan (Social Media, Networking, Advertising, etc.)

Persistence will always reward you

SKILLS
WEEK 5

Working with buyers can be a lot of fun as well as a lot of work. Week 5 focuses on best practices, tips, and tricks on how to work with buyers. It includes items such as gaining buyer agency commitment, controlling your calendar with buyers, as well as mastering your buyer consultation so you can be more efficient and create raving fans.

WEEK 5 | ACTIVITIES: WORKING WITH BUYERS

WHERE	ACTIVITY	RESOURCE	WORKSHEETS	✓
Task	**HOLD 2** Breakthrough Open Houses	Appendix	PG 124 - 126: OH Strategies	
Task	**COFFEE OR LUNCH** with at least 2 Core Advocates from your list	TLR Scripts Booklet		
Task	**UPDATE** Weekly Calendar	T.R.A.C.K. Workbook	PG 60 - 61	
Task	**MAKE** a minimum of 50 Contacts #TLRTenADay	Activity Tracker TLR Scripts Booklet Booklet	PG 59	
Task	**WRITE 10** handwritten notes	TLR Scripts Booklet Booklet		
Task	**ADD 25** people to Database	Activity Tracker	PG 59	
Task	**SET 2** new appointments	Activity Tracker	PG 59	
Task	**SHOOT 1** Facebook Live / Instagram video #TLRNation			
Task	**SCRIPT / ROLE PLAY** at least 15 minutes per day	TLR Scripts Booklet		
Online	**WATCH:** Mindset Minute: Be Intentional (4m)	LockerRoomUniversity.com	Download: KISS Worksheet	
Online	**WATCH:** Buyer Consult Series: Intro (2m)	LockerRoomUniversity.com		
Online	**WATCH & COMPLETE:** Buyer Consult Series: Why We Do One (5m)	LockerRoomUniversity.com	PG 62: Why We Do One	
Online	**WATCH & COMPLETE:** Buyer Consult Series: What Goes Into The Packet (9m)	LockerRoomUniversity.com	PG 63: What Goes Into The Packet Download: Buyer Needs Analysis	
Online	**WATCH & COMPLETE:** Buyer Consult Series: Develop Your Value Proposition (6m)	LockerRoomUniversity.com	PG 62: Develop My Value Proposition	
Online	**WATCH:** Buyer Consult Series: What To Say Before The Appt (2m)	Appendix LockerRoomUniversity.com	Download: Buyer Leads Sheet	
Online	**WATCH:** Buyer Consult Series: What To Say During The Appt (10m)	LockerRoomUniversity.com		
Online	**WATCH:** Buyer Consult Series: Ask For The Agreement (2m)	LockerRoomUniversity.com		
Online	**WATCH:** Buyer Consult Series: Set Expectations Showing Property (3m)	LockerRoomUniversity.com		
Online	**WATCH & LEARN:** The Buyer Consultation Role Play (37m)	LockerRoomUniversity.com		
Task	**CREATE/REFINE/PREPARE:** Your Buyer Consultation	Buyer Consultation Role Play Video & TLR Scripts Booklet	Download: Customizable Buyer Consultation PPT	
Challenge	**PRACTICE/ROLE PLAY:** A Buyer Presentation with a Top Producer or Coach in the Office	TLR Scripts Booklet		

ACTIVITY TRACKER - DATES: _____

	MON	TUES	WED	THURS	FRI	SAT	SUN	ACTUAL	GOAL	TOTAL
ACTIVITIES										
Contacts Made										
Contacts Added to Database										
FSBO Contacts Made										
Expired Contacts Made										
Social Media Contacts Made										
# of Handwritten Notes										
# of Open Houses Held										
# of Doors Knocked										
# of Minutes Script Practicing										
BUSINESS										
Buyer Appointments Held										
Buyer Agency Agreements Signed										
Accepted Buyer Contracts Written										
New Listing Appointments Held										
New Listings Taken										
New Closings From Buyers										
New Closings From Sellers										
Total Closed Volume (Buyer + Seller)										

NOTES / AHA'S

WEEK 5 Calendar

MONDAY _____	TUESDAY _____	WEDNESDAY _____
PRIORITIES	**PRIORITIES**	**PRIORITIES**
1.	1.	1.
2.	2.	2.
3.	3.	3.
6:00AM	6:00AM	6:00AM
7:00AM	7:00AM	7:00AM
8:00AM	8:00AM	8:00AM
9:00AM	9:00AM	9:00AM
10:00AM	10:00AM	10:00AM
11:00AM	11:00AM	11:00AM
12:00AM	12:00AM	12:00AM
1:00PM	1:00PM	1:00PM
2:00PM	2:00PM	2:00PM
3:00PM	3:00PM	3:00PM
4:00PM	4:00PM	4:00PM
5:00PM	5:00PM	5:00PM
6:00PM	6:00PM	6:00PM
7:00PM	7:00PM	7:00PM
8:00PM	8:00PM	8:00PM

CALENDAR HOW TO:

1ST: Personal & Family Time
Date Night, Vacations, Birthdays, etc.

2ND: Events & Other Immovable Things
Lead Gen, Coaching Calls, Trainings, etc.

3RD: Predetermined Appointment Slots
Listing Appts, Showings, Open Houses etc.

4TH: Everything Else
TRACK Activities, Follow up, Transaction Work, Emails, etc.

CURRENT PENDINGS

SELLERS	NOTES / TO DO

BUYERS	NOTES / TO DO

THURSDAY	FRIDAY	SATURDAY
PRIORITIES	**PRIORITIES**	8:00AM
1.	1.	9:00AM
2.	2.	10:00AM
3.	3.	11:00AM
6:00AM	6:00AM	12:00AM
7:00AM	7:00AM	1:00PM
8:00AM	8:00AM	2:00PM
9:00AM	9:00AM	3:00PM
10:00AM	10:00AM	4:00PM
11:00AM	11:00AM	5:00PM
12:00AM	12:00AM	6:00PM
1:00PM	1:00PM	7:00PM
2:00PM	2:00PM	8:00PM
3:00PM	3:00PM	**SUNDAY**
4:00PM	4:00PM	8:00AM
5:00PM	5:00PM	9:00AM
6:00PM	6:00PM	10:00AM
7:00PM	7:00PM	11:00AM
8:00PM	8:00PM	12:00AM
MUST DO		1:00PM
		2:00PM
		3:00PM
		4:00PM
		5:00PM
		6:00PM
		7:00PM
		8:00PM

BUYER CONSULT SERIES: WHY WE DO ONE
Why Consultations Matter

1. Establish yourself as a PROFESSIONAL

2. DISCOVER if you are a good fit

3. Discover the buyer's MOTIVATION

4. Find out the buyer's BIG WHY

BUYER CONSULT SERIES: DEVELOP YOUR VALUE PROPOSITION
Be Real, Be You

1. What words would you use to describe yourself?

2. What words would other people use to describe you?

3. What skills and experiences do you have that make you unique?

4. Write the answers from the above questions into paragraph form.

BUYER CONSULT SERIES: WHAT GOES INTO THE PACKET

Suggested Contents

1. _____
2. _____
3. _____
4. _____
5. _____
6. _____

CONTENT IDEAS:

- Welcome Letter
- Business Card
- Introduction
- Pledge of Quality
- Company Culture
- Testimonials
- FAQs
- Reasons to Buy a Home
- Chamber of Commerce info
- Local Attractions
- Parks and Kid Activities
- Financial Worksheet
- Items Required for Loan Application
- Credit Check Request
- Interest Rate Chart
- Points on a Loan Buying Process
- Mistakes to Avoid
- Steps to Making an Offer
- Information on Schools (if applicable)
- Timeline on the Buying Process
- Pricing Trends
- Price Ranges
- Neighborhood Info
- Profiles
- Inspectors
- Service Providers
- Title Search
- Closing on a Home
- Agency Disclosures
- Utility Guide
- Moving Tips
- Property Notes
- Maps with Names of Neighborhoods & Zip Codes

Real Estate

IS MY HUSTLE

SKILLS
WEEK 6

This week, you will be asked to identify your ideal client so you know who to target with your lead generation and marketing efforts. Additionally, we will dive into what it takes to build trust and articulate your value as a real estate professional. This will allow you to attract the right clients into your sphere of influence so you can build a long term relationship.

WEEK 6 | ACTIVITIES: IDEAL CLIENT, TRUST, AND VALUE

WHERE	ACTIVITY	RESOURCE	WORKSHEETS	✓
Task	**PRACTICE/ROLE PLAY** Objection Handling	TLR Scripts Booklet		
Task	**HOLD 2** Breakthrough Open Houses	Appendix	PG 124-126: Breakthrough Open House Strategies	
Task	**COFFEE OR LUNCH** with at least 2 Core Advocates from your list	Weekly Planner TLR Scripts Booklet		
Task	**UPDATE** Weekly Calendar	T.R.A.C.K. Workbook	PG 68-69	
Task	**MAKE** a minimum of 50 Contacts #TLRTenADay	Activity Tracker TLR Scripts Booklet	PG 67	
Task	**WRITE 10** handwritten notes	Activity Tracker TLR Scripts Booklet	PG 67	
Task	**ADD 25** people to Database	Activity Tracker	PG 67	
Task	**SET 2** new appointments	Activity Tracker	PG 67	
Task	**SHOOT 1** Facebook Live / Instagram video #TLRNation			
Challenge	**WEEKLY CHALLENGE: DOOR KNOCKING** Knock on 25 Doors	TLR Scripts Booklet	PG 73-75	
Online	**WATCH & COMPLETE:** Mindset Minute: Go for No (3m)	LockerRoomUniversity.com		
Online	**WATCH & COMPLETE:** Objection Handling (10m)	LockerRoomUniversity.com	PG 70	
Online	**WATCH & COMPLETE:** Finding Your Niche Market & Ideal Client (15m)	LockerRoomUniversity.com	PG 71-72	
Online	**WATCH & COMPLETE:** Building Trust & Communicating Value (3m)	LockerRoomUniversity.com	PG 71	
Online	**WATCH:** How To Build Trust (12m)	LockerRoomUniversity.com	PG 71	
Online	**WATCH:** Know Your Value & Communicate it Clearly (16m)	LockerRoomUniversity.com	PG 71	
Online	**WATCH:** Trust & Value Closing Thoughts (2m)	LockerRoomUniversity.com		
Task	**COMPLETE** Skills Section Goal Assessment		PG 76	

ACTIVITY TRACKER - DATES: _____

	MON	TUES	WED	THURS	FRI	SAT	SUN	ACTUAL	GOAL	TOTAL
ACTIVITIES										
Contacts Made										
Contacts Added to Database										
FSBO Contacts Made										
Expired Contacts Made										
Social Media Contacts Made										
# of Handwritten Notes										
# of Open Houses Held										
# of Doors Knocked										
# of Minutes Script Practicing										
BUSINESS										
Buyer Appointments Held										
Buyer Agency Agreements Signed										
Accepted Buyer Contracts Written										
New Listing Appointments Held										
New Listings Taken										
New Closings From Buyers										
New Closings From Sellers										
Total Closed Volume (Buyer + Seller)										

NOTES / AHA'S

WEEK 6 Calendar

MONDAY _____	TUESDAY _____	WEDNESDAY _____
PRIORITIES	**PRIORITIES**	**PRIORITIES**
1.	1.	1.
2.	2.	2.
3.	3.	3.
6:00AM	6:00AM	6:00AM
7:00AM	7:00AM	7:00AM
8:00AM	8:00AM	8:00AM
9:00AM	9:00AM	9:00AM
10:00AM	10:00AM	10:00AM
11:00AM	11:00AM	11:00AM
12:00AM	12:00AM	12:00AM
1:00PM	1:00PM	1:00PM
2:00PM	2:00PM	2:00PM
3:00PM	3:00PM	3:00PM
4:00PM	4:00PM	4:00PM
5:00PM	5:00PM	5:00PM
6:00PM	6:00PM	6:00PM
7:00PM	7:00PM	7:00PM
8:00PM	8:00PM	8:00PM

CALENDAR HOW TO:

1ST: Personal & Family Time
Date Night, Vacations, Birthdays, etc.

2ND: Events & Other Immovable Things
Lead Gen, Coaching Calls, Trainings, etc.

3RD: Predetermined Appointment Slots
Listing Appts, Showings, Open Houses etc.

4TH: Everything Else
TRACK Activities, Follow up, Transaction Work, Emails, etc.

CURRENT PENDINGS

SELLERS	NOTES / TO DO

BUYERS	NOTES / TO DO

THURSDAY	FRIDAY	SATURDAY
PRIORITIES	**PRIORITIES**	8:00AM
1.	1.	9:00AM
2.	2.	10:00AM
3.	3.	11:00AM
6:00AM	6:00AM	12:00AM
7:00AM	7:00AM	1:00PM
8:00AM	8:00AM	2:00PM
9:00AM	9:00AM	3:00PM
10:00AM	10:00AM	4:00PM
11:00AM	11:00AM	5:00PM
12:00AM	12:00AM	6:00PM
1:00PM	1:00PM	7:00PM
2:00PM	2:00PM	8:00PM
3:00PM	3:00PM	**SUNDAY**
4:00PM	4:00PM	8:00AM
5:00PM	5:00PM	9:00AM
6:00PM	6:00PM	10:00AM
7:00PM	7:00PM	11:00AM
8:00PM	8:00PM	12:00AM
MUST DO		1:00PM
		2:00PM
		3:00PM
		4:00PM
		5:00PM
		6:00PM
		7:00PM
		8:00PM

OBJECTION HANDLING
Prepare Responses To Common Rebuttals

Objection: _____.

1. Simplify _____

2. Be _____

GO FOR NO

This concept was inspired by the book "Go for No" by Richard Fenton and Andrea Waltz. We often hear how success leaves clues, and yet so does failure. Let me ask you a question, have you learned more from your past successes and wins or have you actually learned more from your failures and losses? It's important to understand that failing and being a "failure" are two very different things. We must learn to celebrate our victories but also be okay with celebrating our failures, knowing it's a learning experience and brings us one step closer to a resounding, YES! In real estate, many agents are allowing their short term fear of hearing the word "No" paralyze them from doing the work it takes to build momentum and be successful.

So this week, we are going to challenge you to Go For No! How many No's do you need to hear before you get to that one Yes? Is it worth it? What if you learned to celebrate hearing the word "No" by knowing it gets you one step closer to the "YES"? Would that change the way you go about doing your business? Would it change the conversations you're having on a daily basis?

If you want it bad enough, you'll find a way. If not, then you'll find an excuse. Go out and collect as many No's as you can! Real estate is a contact sport, it's time to get your jersey dirty.

FINDING YOUR NICHE & IDEAL CLIENT
Why A Niche Is Important:

1. _____
2. _____ vs.
3. _____ of choice

IDENTIFY: _____ and _____

HOW TO BUILD TRUST & COMMUNICATE VALUE
Customer Trust And Loyalty Are Essential For Success.

HOW TO BUILD TRUST

1. Asking _____.
2. Confidence through _____.
3. Being _____.
4. _____.

"The person _____ of the conversation is asking the most questions.
The person that is _____ is doing the most talking."

HOW TO COMMUNICATE WHAT YOU DO (ELEVATOR SPEECH):

1. _____
2. _____
3. _____
4. _____

FORMULATE YOUR ELEVATOR SPEECH:

"I am a _____
and I help _____
achieve _____
so that _____."

IDEAL CLIENT AVATAR
Best-Case Customer Profile

IDEAL CLIENT AVATAR

Buyer/Seller:

Location/Area:

Price Point:

POSSIBLE NICHE:
- ☐ Residential
- ☐ Commercial
- ☐ First Time Homebuyer
- ☐ Luxury
- ☐ New Home Construction
- ☐ Senior Transition/Empty Nesters
- ☐ Estate Sales
- ☐ Farm/Ranch
- ☐ Vacation Homes
- ☐ FSBO
- ☐ Expired
- ☐ Investors
- ☐ Foreclosures
- ☐ Short Sales
- ☐ Divorce

CHALLENGES & PAIN POINTS

Challenges:

Other Pain Points:

POSSIBLE OBJECTIONS

Possible Objections:

GOALS & VALUES

Goals:

Values:

SOURCES OF INFORMATION

Books/Magazines:

Blogs/Websites:

Social Media Accounts:

Seminars:

Other:

WEEKLY CHALLENGE: DOOR KNOCKING - KNOCK ON 25 DOORS IN A NEIGHBORHOOD OR DEMOGRAPHIC YOU WANT TO FARM

Step 1: Preparing for Door Knocking | *It's All in the Details*

Before you go out and knock on doors you have to do a little planning. Where to knock should be a well thought out process.

- Is there a neighborhood you like working? Are you targeting a certain price point? Establish the boundaries of what you consider to be the farm.
- Pull up your MLS and find the number of listings and sales for the most recent 6 to 12-month period within those boundaries.
- Divide the total listings by total homes to get a turnover rate. Ideally, a farm will have a 4% + turnover rate. A well-established listing agent will capture 8% - 15% of those listings.

Example: 24 (listings sold) ÷ 600 (homes) = .04 (4% turnover rate). Agent captures 8% of 24 listings = 2 listings. Once you have identified your area to door knock you'll want to prepare your flyer.

Step 2: How to Door Knock | *What should you do and say?*

Like the Nike campaign says, "Just Do It!". It all starts by knocking on that first door. The good news is...the person opening your first door of the day doesn't know it's your first door of the day. **GO FOR NO!**

Door Knocking Technique:

- Say the affirmation – "I am getting a listing today."
- Knock or ring doorbell.
- Put a smile on your face.
- Have a good attitude and high energy.
- When person answers the door – take a big step back. (It immediately eliminates the fear that you are there to cause harm or intimidate them.)
- Greet the person warmly and go into your script while handing them your flyer.
- Hopefully, schedule an appointment or receive a referral AND be sure to thank them for their time.

SCRIPTS: See the TLR Scripts Simplified Booklet for suggested door knocking scripts!

Step 3: Develop a Listing Agent Mindset | *Smile, Have Good Energy, Listen*

To put yourself in the right frame of mind to attract and capture listings, you'll need to have a listing agent mindset. You'll need a good attitude, a big smile, and great energy.

Let's talk attitude. People can hear it, see it and feel it. They will respond to a positive (and negative for that matter) attitude consciously and subconsciously. If you put on a BIG smile and exude a positive "This IS my neighborhood" attitude, you'll likely get the same back from them. On the flip side, if you go in with a negative attitude, or feel like you don't belong there, you'll get a lot of NO's and maybe a door slammed in your face. What you put out there is mirrored back to you. If you feel great about what you're doing, they will respond with a smile. If you feel uneasy, they will feel uneasy about you.

Think of someone you know who radiates confidence. Think about the way they look, the way they talk, the way they stand. Mimic that attitude and confidence when you go out to door knock!

Don't forget to SMILE big. One of the greatest secrets to success is to smile when you talk. Before you knock on the door, imagine yourself as the Mega Agent for your office. You already have a ton of listings you've gotten from door knocking. You OWN that neighborhood.

Have BIG energy. People can feel your energy. Speak with confidence and shine! Be positive and upbeat. Even when they say "I don't know anyone". Respond with – "Well, when you think of someone, please keep me in mind!"

Lastly, LISTEN more than you talk. Sometimes we get so carried away with remembering to say everything in our script that we forget to listen.

Step 4: What Should I Wear? | *Comfortable, but Professional is the Key*

For all practicality, when door knocking you should dress professionally. This does not mean decked out in your Sunday finest necessarily. Dressing in business casual is usually acceptable.

The most important thing is to wear super comfortable shoes! Black tennis shoes or comfortable slip on loafers work well. The point is, you're not out to win any fashion awards, you want to be able to make money by being able to door knock more homes in the least amount of time. The key to that is comfortable shoes! Your feet will thank you later.

Other necessities are:

- ✗ Clipboard for holding flyers, business cards, and a notepad.
- ✗ Do not carry a bag – for safety reasons
- ✗ Bring a cell phone for security.
- ✗ Always wear a name tag.
- ✗ Some agents wear a lanyard around their neck with their business cards in it and a lock box key card.

Step 5: What Should I Hand Out? | *Flyers, Postcards, and Newsletters...Oh My!*

When door knocking you always want to give something of value to the occupant. Whether it is a CMA of the neighborhood (we don't recommend giving out a full CMA, just a couple "actives" or "recently solds" – you want them to call you for an appointment to get the full CMA) or Just Listed or Just Sold information. You can also give them an invitation to an Open House that you or someone in your office is having that weekend.

You can put a calendar of events or community information on the back of the flyer.

However, the best thing we've found to hand out to occupants are requests for donations – either food or toys. We staple a flyer to a paper bag with "Donations" for a Food or Toy Drive or local Humane Society. This is great to do in concert with back to school, during Thanksgiving or Christmas, or even year-round.

DOOR KNOCKING FAQS
More Tips To Help You

WHAT IS THE BEST TIME OF DAY TO DOOR KNOCK?

We have found the percentage of door knocks answered are about the same whether knocked in the morning, afternoon or early evenings. For 50 doors knocked, we get around 45- 50% answered. We typically see more stay at home parents, retirees, and work from home occupants during the day. Early evenings, you will reach the people who work during the day. Early morning works best on Saturday – before people get up and moving. Try different days and times and see what works best for you.

IS DOOR KNOCKING LEGAL?

Check with local ordinances in your area to be sure (or ask your broker). A permit may be required. However, we've found that coming from a place of contribution partnering with a local charity to also collect food or toy donations, can increase your chances of a positive interaction.

HOW DO I KEEP TRACK OF DOORS I'VE KNOCKED?

We know of agents who use a free app called Spotio. It keeps track of all the houses you've knocked by putting a pin on each house. Then you can assign each house a tag – Not Home, Not Interested, or Lead. There is also a section to put notes on each lead. Every week it will send you a summary of door knocks that week. There are other apps out there that are geared to Door Knockers. Try them out – you'll find what works best for you. Or you can do the old-fashioned way by printing out a plot of the neighborhood and hand write the notes.

HOW DO HOME-OWNERS REACT?

For the most part they are nice and friendly. We love the helpful neighbors and the "busy body" neighbors. They are the ones you want to talk to, and there is usually one or two in each neighborhood. They know everyone's business such as who is moving and who needs to buy or sell. You will meet some people who react negatively or just plain rude. Ignore those people. You don't know what is going on in their day. The negative or rude people may very well be nice people, they just had a bad day and are taking it out on you. Go move on to the next door. However, we've found that coming from a place of contribution partnering with a local charity to also collect food or toy donations can increase your chances of a positive interaction.

Is your jersey dirty yet?

CONGRATS! YOU FINISHED THE SKILLS SECTION OF T.R.A.C.K.!
SKILLS SECTION GOAL ASSESSMENT (WEEKS 4 - 6)

The goal for the end of the Skills section was to be on the path towards mastery and fully equipped with the skills and tools required to identify blind spots and convert business at a high level.

DONE	ACTIVITY
	Create/Perfect Listing Presentation
	Create/Perfect Buyer Consultation
	Ideal Client Established
	175 Contacts Made (Including Door Knocking)
	75 Contacts Added to Database
	6 Appointments Held
	6 Open Houses Held
	30 Handwritten Notes
	6 Coffee or Lunch Dates with Core Advocates or Preferred Vendors

REFLECT AND WRITE YOUR AHA'S FROM THE SKILLS SECTION (WEEKS 4-6):

It's Halftime! Huddle Up!

SYSTEMS
WEEK 7

Week 7 begins the focus on developing Systems for your business. With your activities and focus high up to this point, we want to make sure you implement strong systems for follow up. After all, fortune is in the follow up! It is time to begin working ON your business, not just working IN your business.

WEEK 7 | ACTIVITIES: FOLLOW UP

WHERE	ACTIVITY	RESOURCE	WORKSHEETS	✓
Task	**UPDATE** Weekly Calendar	T.R.A.C.K. Workbook	PG 80-81	
Task	**HOLD 2** Breakthrough Open Houses	Appendix	PG 124 - 126: Breakthrough Open House Strategies	
Task	**COFFEE OR LUNCH** with at least 2 Core Advocates from your list	Weekly Planner TLR Scripts Booklet		
Task	**MAKE** a minimum of 50 Contacts #TLRTenADay	Activity Tracker TLR Scripts Booklet	PG 79	
Task	**WRITE 10** handwritten notes	TLR Scripts Booklet	PG 79	
Task	**ADD 20** people to Database	Activity Tracker	PG 79	
Task	**SET 2** new appointments	Activity Tracker	PG 79	
Task	**SHOOT 1** Facebook Live / Instagram video #TLRNation			
Task	**SCRIPT / ROLE PLAY** at least 15 minutes per day	Activity Tracker TLR Scripts Booklet	PG 79	
Challenge	**WEEKLY CHALLENGE:** Follow Up With 25 Database Contacts Using a New Strategy	TLR Scripts Booklet	PG 83-84	
Online	**WATCH:** Introduction to the Systems Section (2m)	LockerRoomUniversity.com		
Online	**WATCH:** Mindset Minute: Fortune is in the Follow Up (3m)	LockerRoomUniversity.com		
Online	**WATCH & COMPLETE:** Mastering Follow Up (7m)	LockerRoomUniversity.com	PG 82: Mastering Follow Up	
Online	**VISIT** The Facebook Group & interact with our community	facebook.com/groups/LockerRoomNation		

ACTIVITY TRACKER - DATES: _____

	MON	TUES	WED	THURS	FRI	SAT	SUN	ACTUAL	GOAL	TOTAL
ACTIVITIES										
Contacts Made										
Contacts Added to Database										
FSBO Contacts Made										
Expired Contacts Made										
Social Media Contacts Made										
# of Handwritten Notes										
# of Open Houses Held										
# of Doors Knocked										
# of Minutes Script Practicing										
BUSINESS										
Buyer Appointments Held										
Buyer Agency Agreements Signed										
Accepted Buyer Contracts Written										
New Listing Appointments Held										
New Listings Taken										
New Closings From Buyers										
New Closings From Sellers										
Total Closed Volume (Buyer + Seller)										

NOTES / AHA'S

WEEK 7 Calendar

MONDAY	TUESDAY	WEDNESDAY
PRIORITIES	**PRIORITIES**	**PRIORITIES**
1.	1.	1.
2.	2.	2.
3.	3.	3.
6:00AM	6:00AM	6:00AM
7:00AM	7:00AM	7:00AM
8:00AM	8:00AM	8:00AM
9:00AM	9:00AM	9:00AM
10:00AM	10:00AM	10:00AM
11:00AM	11:00AM	11:00AM
12:00AM	12:00AM	12:00AM
1:00PM	1:00PM	1:00PM
2:00PM	2:00PM	2:00PM
3:00PM	3:00PM	3:00PM
4:00PM	4:00PM	4:00PM
5:00PM	5:00PM	5:00PM
6:00PM	6:00PM	6:00PM
7:00PM	7:00PM	7:00PM
8:00PM	8:00PM	8:00PM

CALENDAR HOW TO:	CURRENT PENDINGS	
	SELLERS	NOTES / TO DO
1ST: Personal & Family Time *Date Night, Vacations, Birthdays, etc.*		
2ND: Events & Other Immovable Things *Lead Gen, Coaching Calls, Trainings, etc.*		
	BUYERS	NOTES / TO DO
3RD: Predetermined Appointment Slots *Listing Appts, Showings, Open Houses etc.*		
4TH: Everything Else *TRACK Activities, Follow up, Transaction Work, Emails, etc.*		

THURSDAY _____	FRIDAY _____	SATURDAY _____
PRIORITIES	**PRIORITIES**	8:00AM
1.	1.	9:00AM
2.	2.	10:00AM
3.	3.	11:00AM
6:00AM	6:00AM	12:00AM
7:00AM	7:00AM	1:00PM
8:00AM	8:00AM	2:00PM
9:00AM	9:00AM	3:00PM
10:00AM	10:00AM	4:00PM
11:00AM	11:00AM	5:00PM
12:00AM	12:00AM	6:00PM
1:00PM	1:00PM	7:00PM
2:00PM	2:00PM	8:00PM
3:00PM	3:00PM	**SUNDAY** _____
4:00PM	4:00PM	8:00AM
5:00PM	5:00PM	9:00AM
6:00PM	6:00PM	10:00AM
7:00PM	7:00PM	11:00AM
8:00PM	8:00PM	12:00AM

MUST DO		Sunday cont.
		1:00PM
		2:00PM
		3:00PM
		4:00PM
		5:00PM
		6:00PM
		7:00PM
		8:00PM

WWW.TLRNATION.COM

MASTERING FOLLOW UP
Keep Fishing For Your Clients

92% of real estate agents give up after four "nos", and only 8% of them ask for the appointment a fifth time. When you consider that 80% of prospects say "no" four times before they say "yes", this suggests that 8% of sales people are getting 80% of the sales. Which one are you? **LET'S GO FOR NO!!**

It takes an average of _____ cold call attempts to reach a prospect.

The best time to call is between _____ and _____.

_____% to _____% of sales go to the agent that is the first to follow up.

_____% of agents that use social media out perform agents that do not.

However, _____ is almost _____ times more effective than social media.

Agents who ask for referrals earn _____ to _____ times more than agents that do not.

PRO TIP: UTILIZE A 31 DAY FOLLOW UP SYSTEM

This low tech follow-up system works because it eliminates distractions that come with an online CRM, like email and scrolling through social media. Find a quiet space, place a do not disturb sign on the door, and use an office landline if possible to avoid distractions on your phone.

WHAT YOU'LL NEED:
- Desktop file holder or filing cabinet
- 31 file dividers
- Divider labels
- Buyer & Seller Lead Sheets

WHAT TO DO:

1. Label your file dividers 1-31 to correspond with the maximum 31 days in a month.

2. Place the dividers into your cabinet or desktop file holder in order of 1-31.

3. As you lead generate, utilize the Buyer and Seller Lead Sheets found in the appendix. After you have made a contact/call, write the date and notes on the back of the lead sheet and place it in the next file folder that corresponds with the day you would like to make your next follow up contact.

   Example: **NOTE: 6/1 - Spoke with Tom. Says spouse will be home from work trip next week, follow up in 2 weeks.**

   Then place the lead sheet in the file folder labeled 15, representing the 15th day of the month.

4. If the date falls on a weekend, make those calls on Monday if you'd like. Once you reach the end of the month, start over! If you have an admin, instruct them to enter notes into a CRM at the end of each week.

WEEKLY CHALLENGE: UP YOUR FOLLOW UP GAME
FOLLOW UP WITH 25 DATABASE CONTACTS USING A NEW STRATEGY

1. IDENTIFY YOUR 25 CONTACTS

2. PLAN OUT YOUR FOLLOW UP DATES AND THE STRATEGY

HERE ARE SOME IDEAS TO GET YOU STARTED:

- Create a Market Report and upload to YouTube, Facebook, or Instagram
- Offer a Free Home Valuation
- Text information about a local event to a contact group in that region/neighborhood
- Personal text or video message
- Pop By
- Phone call coming from contribution or value to contact
- Phone call or text asking who they know that does good landscaping, home improvements, etc.
- Handwritten note
- Put all buyers on a market search report
- Add contacts to an email outreach plan
- Create a "hidden gems" report for their area (best restaurants, beaches, shops, etc.)
- Organize a community service project and invite your contacts

FORTUNE IS IN THE FOLLOW UP
Up Your Follow Up Game

Name / Address	1	2	3	4	WHERE THE MAGIC HAPPENS					
					5	6	7	8	9	10

SYSTEMS
WEEK 8

People don't necessarily remember what you say, however people do remember how you make them feel. Week 8 is all about the client experience. You will dive into creating your client experience campaign in order to deliver a 10+ experience for every client you work with. By building this system, you are sure to create a relationship and referral based business.

WEEK 8 | ACTIVITIES: CLIENT EXPERIENCE

WHERE	ACTIVITY	RESOURCE	WORKSHEETS	✓
Task	**UPDATE** Weekly Calendar	T.R.A.C.K. Workbook	PG 88-89	
Task	**HOLD 2** Breakthrough Open Houses	Appendix	PG 124 - 126: Breakthrough Open House Strategies	
Task	**COFFEE OR LUNCH** with at least 2 Core Advocates from your list	Weekly Planner TLR Scripts Booklet		
Task	**MAKE** a minimum of 50 Contacts #TLRTenADay	Activity Tracker TLR Scripts Booklet	PG 87	
Task	**WRITE 10** handwritten notes	Activity Tracker TLR Scripts Booklet	PG 87	
Task	**ADD 20** people to Database	Activity Tracker	PG 87	
Task	**SET 2** new appointments	Activity Tracker	PG 87	
Task	**SHOOT 1** Facebook Live / Instagram video #TLRNation			
Task	**SCRIPT / ROLE PLAY** at least 15 minutes per day	TLR Scripts Booklet		
Online	**WATCH:** Mindset Minute: Do Sweat the Small Stuff (2m)	LockerRoomUniversity.com		
Online	**WATCH & COMPLETE:** The Client Experience Campaign (16m)	LockerRoomUniversity.com	PG 90: Creating Your Client Experience Campaign	
Task	**CREATE & IMPLEMENT:** Your Client Experience Campaign	12 Month Blank Calendar Client Experience Ideas	PG 90-92 Client Experience Campaign Planning and Examples	
Challenge	**WEEKLY CHALLENGE: SCHEDULE** a Minimum of 10 pop by's	Client Experience Ideas Pop By Ideas	PG 91-92	
Online	**VISIT** The Facebook Group & interact with our community	facebook.com/groups/LockerRoomNation		

ACTIVITY TRACKER - DATES: _____

ACTIVITIES

	MON	TUES	WED	THURS	FRI	SAT	SUN	ACTUAL	GOAL	TOTAL
Contacts Made										
Contacts Added to Database										
FSBO Contacts Made										
Expired Contacts Made										
Social Media Contacts Made										
# of Handwritten Notes										
# of Open Houses Held										
# of Doors Knocked										
# of Minutes Script Practicing										

BUSINESS

	MON	TUES	WED	THURS	FRI	SAT	SUN	ACTUAL	GOAL	TOTAL
Buyer Appointments Held										
Buyer Agency Agreements Signed										
Accepted Buyer Contracts Written										
New Listing Appointments Held										
New Listings Taken										
New Closings From Buyers										
New Closings From Sellers										
Total Closed Volume (Buyer + Seller)										

NOTES / AHA'S

WEEK 8 Calendar

MONDAY	TUESDAY	WEDNESDAY
PRIORITIES	**PRIORITIES**	**PRIORITIES**
1.	1.	1.
2.	2.	2.
3.	3.	3.
6:00AM	6:00AM	6:00AM
7:00AM	7:00AM	7:00AM
8:00AM	8:00AM	8:00AM
9:00AM	9:00AM	9:00AM
10:00AM	10:00AM	10:00AM
11:00AM	11:00AM	11:00AM
12:00AM	12:00AM	12:00AM
1:00PM	1:00PM	1:00PM
2:00PM	2:00PM	2:00PM
3:00PM	3:00PM	3:00PM
4:00PM	4:00PM	4:00PM
5:00PM	5:00PM	5:00PM
6:00PM	6:00PM	6:00PM
7:00PM	7:00PM	7:00PM
8:00PM	8:00PM	8:00PM

CALENDAR HOW TO:

1ST: Personal & Family Time
Date Night, Vacations, Birthdays, etc.

2ND: Events & Other Immovable Things
Lead Gen, Coaching Calls, Trainings, etc.

3RD: Predetermined Appointment Slots
Listing Appts, Showings, Open Houses etc.

4TH: Everything Else
TRACK Activities, Follow up, Transaction Work, Emails, etc.

CURRENT PENDINGS

SELLERS	NOTES / TO DO

BUYERS	NOTES / TO DO

THURSDAY _____	FRIDAY _____	SATURDAY _____
PRIORITIES	**PRIORITIES**	8:00AM
1.	1.	9:00AM
2.	2.	10:00AM
3.	3.	11:00AM
6:00AM	6:00AM	12:00AM
7:00AM	7:00AM	1:00PM
8:00AM	8:00AM	2:00PM
9:00AM	9:00AM	3:00PM
10:00AM	10:00AM	4:00PM
11:00AM	11:00AM	5:00PM
12:00AM	12:00AM	6:00PM
1:00PM	1:00PM	7:00PM
2:00PM	2:00PM	8:00PM
3:00PM	3:00PM	**SUNDAY** _____
4:00PM	4:00PM	8:00AM
5:00PM	5:00PM	9:00AM
6:00PM	6:00PM	10:00AM
7:00PM	7:00PM	11:00AM
8:00PM	8:00PM	12:00AM

MUST DO

SUNDAY (cont.)
1:00PM
2:00PM
3:00PM
4:00PM
5:00PM
6:00PM
7:00PM
8:00PM

WWW.TLRNATION.COM

CLIENT EXPERIENCE CAMPAIGN - GROW YOUR "CLUB"
What Interactions Are Your Clients Engaging In?

CREATING YOUR CLIENT EXPERIENCE CAMPAIGN

1. _____
2. _____
3. _____
4. _____
5. _____
6. _____

Pro Tip: Creating an out-of-this-world Client Experience Campaign does not have to cost a fortune. Team up with a Preferred Vendor or another agent in the office to split costs and maximize the guest list.

JANUARY	JULY
FEBRUARY	AUGUST
MARCH	SEPTEMBER
APRIL	OCTOBER
MAY	NOVEMBER
JUNE	DECEMBER

CLIENT EXPERIENCE CAMPAIGN
Client Experience Ideas

JANUARY
Winter Home Maintenance Ideas
Calendars

FEBRUARY
Home Matchmaker
Blood Drive

MARCH
March Madness Brackets
Spring Home Prep

APRIL
Flower Seed Packets
Nursery Gift Card Giveaway

MAY
Memorial Day Flags
Memorial Day Parade

JUNE
Summer Pool Party
Drive-In Theater Customer Appreciation Party

JULY
Sparklers or Flags
Fireworks Watch Party
Fourth of July Parade

AUGUST
Back to School Supply Drive
So Long Summer Pool Party or Cook Out
Ice Cream Social

SEPTEMBER
Local Football Schedules
Football Tailgating

OCTOBER
Trick or Treating Open House
Pumpkin Patch Customer Appreciation Event

NOVEMBER
Thank You Calls
Thanksgiving Pies

DECEMBER
Holiday Client Appreciation Party
Pictures with Santa
Gift Wrapping Day

If you think practice is boring... try sitting on the bench.

CLIENT EXPERIENCE CAMPAIGN
Pop By Ideas For Past Clients and Sphere

"Pop By's," by definition, means to visit a person or a place for a short period because you're just popping by and possibly leaving them an item of value.

WINTER
GIFT WRAP POP BY

- Roll of Wrapping Paper/Gift Wrap
- Clear Tape
- Witty Script: *"I'm wrapping up another great year in real estate thanks to awesome clients like you! Thank you for your business or referral!"*

SPRING
FARMER'S MARKET

- Reusable Shopping Bag/Tote (Brand it!)
- Local Farmers Market Schedule
- Witty Script: *"Reduce, Recycle, Re-use me as your Realtor"*

SUMMER
FAVORITE BBQ SAUCE OR RUB

- Favorite Sauce or Rub
- Witty Script: *"Friends don't let friends eat crappy BBQ... or buy or sell a home without a seasoned real estate agent! Your referrals are my business's secret sauce"*

FALL
CARAMEL APPLE KIT

- Mason Jar
- Caramels
- Popsicle Sticks
- Sprinkles/Toppings
- Witty Script: *"Buying and Selling real estate should be "sweet" and never "sticky!" I am never too busy for you and your referrals!"*
- Include Instructions

SYSTEMS
WEEK 9

Are you running your business like a CEO? Week 9 dives into the importance of tracking your numbers in a systematic way. Numbers tell a story and if you're not running your business based on numbers, then that means you are susceptible to the ebb and flow of your emotions on a daily basis. This powerful session breaks down why knowing your numbers is so important and how it will help you run an efficient business.

WEEK 9 | ACTIVITIES: RUNNING YOUR BUSINESS LIKE A BUSINESS

WHERE	ACTIVITY	RESOURCE	WORKSHEETS	✓
Task	UPDATE Weekly Calendar	T.R.A.C.K. Workbook	PG 96-97	
Task	HOLD 2 Breakthrough Open Houses	Appendix	PG 124 - 126: Breakthrough Open House Strategies	
Task	COFFEE OR LUNCH with at least 2 Core Advocates from your list	Weekly Planner TLR Scripts Booklet		
Task	MAKE a minimum of 50 Contacts #TLRTenADay	Activity Tracker TLR Scripts Booklet	PG 95	
Task	WRITE 10 handwritten notes	Activity Tracker TLR Scripts Booklet	PG 95	
Task	ADD 20 people to Database	Activity Tracker	PG 95	
Task	SET 2 new appointments	Activity Tracker	PG 95	
Task	SHOOT 1 Facebook Live / Instagram video #TLRNation			
Task	SCRIPT / ROLE PLAY at least 15 minutes per day	TLR Scripts Booklet		
Online	WATCH: Mindset Minute: Be the CEO of Your Business (3m)	LockerRoomUniversity.com		
Online	WATCH: Numbers Tell a Story (6m)	LockerRoomUniversity.com		
Online	WATCH: Know Your Numbers: A Case Study (21m)	LockerRoomUniversity.com		
Challenge	WEEKLY CHALLENGE: #BETHECEO CHALLENGE		PG 98: Contact Ratios	
Online	VISIT The Facebook Group & interact with our community	facebook.com/groups/LockerRoomNation		
Task	COMPLETE Systems Section Goal Assessment	T.R.A.C.K. Workbook	PG 99	

ACTIVITY TRACKER - DATES: _____

	MON	TUES	WED	THURS	FRI	SAT	SUN	ACTUAL	GOAL	TOTAL
ACTIVITIES										
Contacts Made										
Contacts Added to Database										
FSBO Contacts Made										
Expired Contacts Made										
Social Media Contacts Made										
# of Handwritten Notes										
# of Open Houses Held										
# of Doors Knocked										
# of Minutes Script Practicing										
BUSINESS										
Buyer Appointments Held										
Buyer Agency Agreements Signed										
Accepted Buyer Contracts Written										
New Listing Appointments Held										
New Listings Taken										
New Closings From Buyers										
New Closings From Sellers										
Total Closed Volume (Buyer + Seller)										

NOTES / AHA'S

WEEK 9 Calendar

MONDAY	TUESDAY	WEDNESDAY
PRIORITIES	**PRIORITIES**	**PRIORITIES**
1.	1.	1.
2.	2.	2.
3.	3.	3.
6:00AM	6:00AM	6:00AM
7:00AM	7:00AM	7:00AM
8:00AM	8:00AM	8:00AM
9:00AM	9:00AM	9:00AM
10:00AM	10:00AM	10:00AM
11:00AM	11:00AM	11:00AM
12:00AM	12:00AM	12:00AM
1:00PM	1:00PM	1:00PM
2:00PM	2:00PM	2:00PM
3:00PM	3:00PM	3:00PM
4:00PM	4:00PM	4:00PM
5:00PM	5:00PM	5:00PM
6:00PM	6:00PM	6:00PM
7:00PM	7:00PM	7:00PM
8:00PM	8:00PM	8:00PM

CALENDAR HOW TO:

1ST: Personal & Family Time
Date Night, Vacations, Birthdays, etc.

2ND: Events & Other Immovable Things
Lead Gen, Coaching Calls, Trainings, etc.

3RD: Predetermined Appointment Slots
Listing Appts, Showings, Open Houses etc.

4TH: Everything Else
TRACK Activities, Follow up, Transaction Work, Emails, etc.

CURRENT PENDINGS

SELLERS	NOTES / TO DO

BUYERS	NOTES / TO DO

THURSDAY _____	FRIDAY _____	SATURDAY _____
PRIORITIES	**PRIORITIES**	8:00AM
1.	1.	9:00AM
2.	2.	10:00AM
3.	3.	11:00AM
6:00AM	6:00AM	12:00AM
7:00AM	7:00AM	1:00PM
8:00AM	8:00AM	2:00PM
9:00AM	9:00AM	3:00PM
10:00AM	10:00AM	4:00PM
11:00AM	11:00AM	5:00PM
12:00AM	12:00AM	6:00PM
1:00PM	1:00PM	7:00PM
2:00PM	2:00PM	8:00PM
3:00PM	3:00PM	**SUNDAY _____**
4:00PM	4:00PM	8:00AM
5:00PM	5:00PM	9:00AM
6:00PM	6:00PM	10:00AM
7:00PM	7:00PM	11:00AM
8:00PM	8:00PM	12:00AM

MUST DO	

	1:00PM
	2:00PM
	3:00PM
	4:00PM
	5:00PM
	6:00PM
	7:00PM
	8:00PM

WEEKLY CHALLENGE: #BETHECEO CHALLENGE

Are you acting like a CEO in your business?

LOOK BACK AT YOUR PREVIOUS 8 WEEKS AND CALCULATE:

Total Contacts Made During T.R.A.C.K.:_____

Total Appointments (Buyer + Listing) Held During T.R.A.C.K.:_____

Total Homes Pending / Under Contract:_____

Total Listings Taken:_____

Total Buyer Agency Agreements Signed:_____

CONTACT RATIOS:

Contact to Appointment Ratio

Take the total number of Contacts Made and divide by the total number of Appointments Held (Ex: 500 contacts made ÷ 8 appointments held = 62.5 to 1 Ratio, meaning for every 62.5 conversations you end up getting an appointment)

YOUR TURN: _____

Contacts to New Clients Signed Ratio

Add together the total number of Listings Taken and Buyer Agency Agreements Signed. Now take the total number of Contacts Made and divide by the total number of Listings Taken + Buyer Agency Agreements Signed. (Ex: 500 Contacts ÷ 4 New Business Signed = 125, meaning for every 125 conversations you end up getting a new client signed).

YOUR TURN: _____

Contacts to Pending Sales Ratio

Take the total number of Contacts Made and divide by the total number of Pending Sales that have gone under contract. (Ex: 500 Contacts ÷ 2 Pending Sales = 250, meaning for every 250 conversations you end up getting a new sale under contract).

YOUR TURN: _____

REFLECT:

What is the take away from knowing your numbers?_____

_____

Where do you have the biggest opportunity for improvement moving forward? _____

_____

CONGRATS! YOU FINISHED THE SYSTEMS SECTION OF T.R.A.C.K.!
SYSTEMS SECTION GOAL ASSESSMENT (WEEKS 7 - 9)

The goal for the end of the Systems section was to build and refine your systems in order to work towards higher efficiency and effectiveness so you can work smarter and not necessarily harder.

DONE	ACTIVITY
	Sourced Leads and Calculated ROI
	Established & Implemented a Follow Up Plan
	Planned 12 Month Client Experience Campaign
	10 Pop By's Scheduled and Planned
	150 Contacts
	60 Contacts Added to Database
	6 Appointments Held
	6 Open Houses Held
	30 Handwritten Notes
	6 Coffee or Lunch Dates with Core Advocates or Preferred Vendors
	25 Database Contacts Followed Up With Using a New Strategy
	Contact, Appointment, and Closing Ratios Calculated (#BETHECEO)

REFLECT AND WRITE YOUR AHA'S FROM THE SYSTEMS SECTION (WEEKS 7-9):

Sweat is Necessary to be the Best

THE DREAM IS FREE

The Hustle

IS SOLD SEPARATELY.

ACHIEVEMENT
WEEK 10

Week 10 begins the final phase of our T.R.A.C.K. program and the next few weeks will focus on Achievement. This week will impact you in more ways than one as we dive into creating your story and telling it to others in an authentic and transparent way. It shares a system of how to create your story that leads to stronger and more meaningful relationships.

WEEK 10 | ACTIVITIES: YOUR STORY BRAID

WHERE	ACTIVITY	RESOURCE	WORKSHEETS	✓
Task	**HOLD 2** Breakthrough Open Houses	Appendix	PG 124 - 126: Breakthrough Open House Strategies	
Task	**COFFEE OR LUNCH** with at least 2 Core Advocates from your list	Weekly Planner TLR Scripts Booklet		
Task	**UPDATE** Weekly Calendar	T.R.A.C.K. Workbook	PG 104-105	
Task	**MAKE** a minimum of 50 Contacts #TLRTenADay	Activity Tracker TLR Scripts Booklet	PG 103	
Task	**WRITE 10** handwritten notes	Activity Tracker TLR Scripts Booklet	PG 103	
Task	**ADD 15** people to Database	Activity Tracker	PG 103	
Task	**SET 2** new appointments	Activity Tracker	PG 103	
Task	**SHOOT 1** Facebook Live / Instagram video #TLRNation			
Task	**SCRIPT / ROLE PLAY** at least 15 minutes per day	TLR Scripts Booklet		
Online	**WATCH:** Mindset Minute: Extreme Ownership (2m)	LockerRoomUniversity.com		
Online	**WATCH:** Introduction to the Achievement Section (1m)	LockerRoomUniversity.com		
Online	**WATCH:** Your Story Braid, Craft It, Tell it: Intro (8m)	LockerRoomUniversity.com		
Online	**WATCH:** Your Story Braid, Craft It, Tell It: 6 Human Needs (9m)	LockerRoomUniversity.com		
Online	**WATCH:** Your Story Braid, Craft It, Tell It: The Steps (9m)	LockerRoomUniversity.com		
Online	**WATCH & COMPLETE:** Your Story Braid, Craft It, Tell It: Craft It! (7m)	LockerRoomUniversity.com	PG 106-108: Your Story Braid, Craft It, Tell It: Craft It!	
Online	**WATCH & COMPLETE:** Jake's Story (17m)	LockerRoomUniversity.com		
Challenge	**WEEKLY CHALLENGE:** Tell YOUR Story	T.R.A.C.K. Workbook Create Your Story Worksheets	PG 107-108: Your Story Braid, Craft It, Tell It: Craft It!	

ACTIVITY TRACKER - DATES: _____

	MON	TUES	WED	THURS	FRI	SAT	SUN	ACTUAL	GOAL	TOTAL
ACTIVITIES										
Contacts Made										
Contacts Added to Database										
FSBO Contacts Made										
Expired Contacts Made										
Social Media Contacts Made										
# of Handwritten Notes										
# of Open Houses Held										
# of Doors Knocked										
# of Minutes Script Practicing										
BUSINESS										
Buyer Appointments Held										
Buyer Agency Agreements Signed										
Accepted Buyer Contracts Written										
New Listing Appointments Held										
New Listings Taken										
New Closings From Buyers										
New Closings From Sellers										
Total Closed Volume (Buyer + Seller)										

NOTES / AHA'S

WEEK 10 Calendar

MONDAY	TUESDAY	WEDNESDAY
PRIORITIES	**PRIORITIES**	**PRIORITIES**
1.	1.	1.
2.	2.	2.
3.	3.	3.
6:00AM	6:00AM	6:00AM
7:00AM	7:00AM	7:00AM
8:00AM	8:00AM	8:00AM
9:00AM	9:00AM	9:00AM
10:00AM	10:00AM	10:00AM
11:00AM	11:00AM	11:00AM
12:00AM	12:00AM	12:00AM
1:00PM	1:00PM	1:00PM
2:00PM	2:00PM	2:00PM
3:00PM	3:00PM	3:00PM
4:00PM	4:00PM	4:00PM
5:00PM	5:00PM	5:00PM
6:00PM	6:00PM	6:00PM
7:00PM	7:00PM	7:00PM
8:00PM	8:00PM	8:00PM

CALENDAR HOW TO:

1ST: Personal & Family Time
Date Night, Vacations, Birthdays, etc.

2ND: Events & Other Immovable Things
Lead Gen, Coaching Calls, Trainings, etc.

3RD: Predetermined Appointment Slots
Listing Appts, Showings, Open Houses etc.

4TH: Everything Else
TRACK Activities, Follow up, Transaction Work, Emails, etc.

CURRENT PENDINGS

SELLERS	NOTES / TO DO

BUYERS	NOTES / TO DO

THURSDAY	FRIDAY	SATURDAY
PRIORITIES	**PRIORITIES**	8:00AM
1.	1.	9:00AM
2.	2.	10:00AM
3.	3.	11:00AM
6:00AM	6:00AM	12:00AM
7:00AM	7:00AM	1:00PM
8:00AM	8:00AM	2:00PM
9:00AM	9:00AM	3:00PM
10:00AM	10:00AM	4:00PM
11:00AM	11:00AM	5:00PM
12:00AM	12:00AM	6:00PM
1:00PM	1:00PM	7:00PM
2:00PM	2:00PM	8:00PM
3:00PM	3:00PM	**SUNDAY**
4:00PM	4:00PM	8:00AM
5:00PM	5:00PM	9:00AM
6:00PM	6:00PM	10:00AM
7:00PM	7:00PM	11:00AM
8:00PM	8:00PM	12:00AM

MUST DO

SUNDAY (cont.)
1:00PM
2:00PM
3:00PM
4:00PM
5:00PM
6:00PM
7:00PM
8:00PM

CREATING YOUR STORY BRAID
Craft It, Tell It

STEP 1: WRITING THE "SCRIPT" TO YOUR STORY

Instructions: This is the brainstorming phase in which you flush out defining moments that have led to your success journey. Don't overthink this phase. Create a storyboard where you write down all events, successes, failures, and challenges you overcame that have helped shape who you are today. The goal here is to document all of the moments that allow you to reflect and be vulnerable about sharing as part of your story.

QUESTIONS TO CONSIDER:

- What accomplishment in your personal life are you most proud of?
- What accomplishment in business are you most proud of?
- When is a time someone told you that you couldn't do something?
- Who has been the most influential person in your life that has helped you?
- When did you feel the "tap" on your shoulder that you were meant for greatness?
- Did it always come easy for you?
- What challenges have you had to overcome?
- What was your mindset during the adversity?
- What habits helped shape the person you are today?
- Was there a particular defining moment that helped you get to where you are?
- What circumstances were you in that you got yourself out of?
- Where do you find peace during a whirlwind of chaos?
- What do you wish someone would have told you?
- How did you create momentum?
- What was your greatest failure? What did you learn from it?
- What is your inspiration?
- Was there a specific moment where you made a definitive decision to change your life?

STEP 2: CREATING THE "HIGHLIGHT REEL" TO YOUR MOVIE TRAILER

Instructions: Now that you've listed critical moments in your life that have helped shape you and lead to your breakthrough success, it is time to go back through and highlight the best of the best. This would be the "Movie Trailer" of your story, which flashes the highlights to captivate an audience. Take the most profound moments you've listed and isolate them from the rest, especially with how it relates to your audience, knowing they likely have experienced the same thoughts, feelings, and struggles.

QUESTIONS TO CONSIDER:

- What is the Top 20% most impactful items listed above?
- Which would naturally connect the most with your audience?
- What moments listed above get you the most passionate?
- Why do you want to share these with your audience?
- Who will most likely connect with each of your moments listed?
- What do you hope for your audience to walk away with when they hear your story?
- What moments listed above can you NOT afford to leave out?
- What might someone else tell you that you must include in your story?
- Which would your "old self" find most valuable if you knew then what you know now?

STEP 3: YOUR STORY BRAID

Instructions: It is vital to have a flow to your story, so it connects with the audience. With the highlight reel points chosen, it's time to craft the actual narrative and build emotion. The following four steps are critical to follow when creating the flow of your story and how it all ties together. This sequence should follow from beginning to end: **Heart - Head - Call to Action - Heart**.

1. THE HEART: You want to spend the first 5 minutes connecting with your audience through your authentic story based on Steps 1 & 2. They need to feel connected to you and see themselves inside of your story before we can move them into logic, action, and ending with one more heartfelt tale. Begin to write the narrative below from bullet point form into written story form, so it's packed with emotion and a flow that is easy to follow with the audience.

_____

_____

_____

_____

_____

_____

_____

_____

2. THE HEAD: Now that we've engaged them emotionally, we transition to logic. This piece is your formal presentation where you shared the proprietary steps of how you went from ordinary to extraordinary or what you do differently to market listings. Share your documented systems to show them that, with your help, they can achieve exceptional results. This method may also include showing comparable homes (CMA), what you do differently than most agents, and systematically articulating your unique value proposition.

(Ex: – The 12 step marketing plan I use to sell homes for 99.8% of list price and 27 average days on the market)

_____

_____

_____

_____

_____

_____

CREATING YOUR STORY BRAID
Craft It, Tell It - Continued

3. CALL-TO-ACTION: By now, you've authentically connected with the audience through your story, and you've gained their trust by showing them the efforts you took to achieve success. It's a natural progression for you to "close" them on the next step, so they leave with an action item to complete. For example, ask them to list with you, register for an upcoming appreciation event, or visit your website and watch a video. Whatever the appropriate next step is, the call-to-action needs to clearly instruct them on where to go and what to do next. Our suggestion is to utilize the "stacking" technique by making an offer available to them for a limited time. Ideals for this include doing a free home valuation or offering a free moving truck to assist in their next move. Show the original price it would cost with a line through it and reveal to them the value they can get by taking action today. What are some ideas or questions you can come up with for a call to action?

_____
_____
_____
_____
_____
_____
_____
_____
_____
_____

4. THE HEART: Do not miss this last step. Many people fail because they stop at the third step and exit stage left. You need to connect with the audience one more time by giving one more heartfelt story. 70% of people make emotional buying decisions, so we need to circle back around with a story that connects and humanizes you again. Possibly share another example from your own life or a recent home seller or buyer you've helped overcome all odds, or by working with you, they got the deal of a lifetime. What story will you close out with that evokes an emotion that causes them to act?

_____
_____
_____
_____
_____
_____
_____
_____
_____
_____

ACHIEVEMENT
WEEK 11

How well do you know your market? Week 11 challenges you to be the local economist of choice in your community and especially to your sphere of influence. By knowing the real estate market better than anyone else, this positions you as the expert in the field and it will lead to more business and higher conversions. Are you ready to become a student of the real estate game?

WEEK 11 | ACTIVITIES: BECOME THE LOCAL ECONOMIST OF CHOICE

WHERE	ACTIVITY	RESOURCE	WORKSHEETS	✓
Task	**UPDATE** Weekly Calendar	T.R.A.C.K. Workbook	PG 112-113	
Task	**HOLD 2** Breakthrough Open Houses	Appendix	PG 124 - 126: Breakthrough Open House Strategies	
Task	**COFFEE OR LUNCH** with at least 2 Core Advocates from your list	Weekly Planner TLR Scripts Booklet		
Task	**MAKE** a minimum of 50 Contacts #TLRTenADay	Activity Tracker TLR Scripts Booklet	PG 111	
Task	**WRITE 10** handwritten notes	Activity Tracker LockerRoomUniversity.com	PG 111	
Task	**ADD 15** people to Database	Activity Tracker	PG 111	
Task	**SET 2** new appointments	Activity Tracker	PG 111	
Task	**SHOOT 1** Facebook Live / Instagram video #TLRNation			
Task	**SCRIPT / ROLE PLAY** at least 15 minutes per day	TLR Scripts Booklet		
Challenge	**WEEKLY CHALLENGE:** Research and Share Market Update	LockerRoomUniversity.com		
Online	**WATCH:** Mindset Minute: Be a Student of the Game (2m)	LockerRoomUniversity.com		
Online	**WATCH:** The Local Economist - Top Agent Interview (60m)	LockerRoomUniversity.com		
Online	**WATCH & COMPLETE:** Top Of Mind Awareness (23m)	LockerRoomUniversity.com	PG 114: Top Of Mind Awareness	
Online	**VISIT** The Facebook Group & interact with our community	facebook.com/groups/LockerRoomNation		

ACTIVITY TRACKER - DATES: _____

	MON	TUES	WED	THURS	FRI	SAT	SUN	ACTUAL	GOAL	TOTAL
ACTIVITIES										
Contacts Made										
Contacts Added to Database										
FSBO Contacts Made										
Expired Contacts Made										
Social Media Contacts Made										
# of Handwritten Notes										
# of Open Houses Held										
# of Doors Knocked										
# of Minutes Script Practicing										
BUSINESS										
Buyer Appointments Held										
Buyer Agency Agreements Signed										
Accepted Buyer Contracts Written										
New Listing Appointments Held										
New Listings Taken										
New Closings From Buyers										
New Closings From Sellers										
Total Closed Volume (Buyer + Seller)										

NOTES / AHA'S

WEEK 11 Calendar

MONDAY	TUESDAY	WEDNESDAY
PRIORITIES	**PRIORITIES**	**PRIORITIES**
1.	1.	1.
2.	2.	2.
3.	3.	3.
6:00AM	6:00AM	6:00AM
7:00AM	7:00AM	7:00AM
8:00AM	8:00AM	8:00AM
9:00AM	9:00AM	9:00AM
10:00AM	10:00AM	10:00AM
11:00AM	11:00AM	11:00AM
12:00AM	12:00AM	12:00AM
1:00PM	1:00PM	1:00PM
2:00PM	2:00PM	2:00PM
3:00PM	3:00PM	3:00PM
4:00PM	4:00PM	4:00PM
5:00PM	5:00PM	5:00PM
6:00PM	6:00PM	6:00PM
7:00PM	7:00PM	7:00PM
8:00PM	8:00PM	8:00PM

CALENDAR HOW TO:

1ST: Personal & Family Time
Date Night, Vacations, Birthdays, etc.

2ND: Events & Other Immovable Things
Lead Gen, Coaching Calls, Trainings, etc.

3RD: Predetermined Appointment Slots
Listing Appts, Showings, Open Houses etc.

4TH: Everything Else
TRACK Activities, Follow up, Transaction Work, Emails, etc.

CURRENT PENDINGS

SELLERS	NOTES / TO DO

BUYERS	NOTES / TO DO

THURSDAY _____	FRIDAY _____	SATURDAY _____
PRIORITIES	**PRIORITIES**	8:00AM
1.	1.	9:00AM
2.	2.	10:00AM
3.	3.	11:00AM
6:00AM	6:00AM	12:00AM
7:00AM	7:00AM	1:00PM
8:00AM	8:00AM	2:00PM
9:00AM	9:00AM	3:00PM
10:00AM	10:00AM	4:00PM
11:00AM	11:00AM	5:00PM
12:00AM	12:00AM	6:00PM
1:00PM	1:00PM	7:00PM
2:00PM	2:00PM	8:00PM
3:00PM	3:00PM	**SUNDAY** _____
4:00PM	4:00PM	8:00AM
5:00PM	5:00PM	9:00AM
6:00PM	6:00PM	10:00AM
7:00PM	7:00PM	11:00AM
8:00PM	8:00PM	12:00AM

MUST DO	
	1:00PM
	2:00PM
	3:00PM
	4:00PM
	5:00PM
	6:00PM
	7:00PM
	8:00PM

TOP OF MIND AWARENESS
Be Remembered

Gaining Top of Mind Awareness improves your yield or likely hood of converting the contacts in your database into closed business.

EXAMPLE: Based on 240 people in your database

First-Year Yield

5% conversion = _____ units in closed business

Second-Year Yield

10% conversion = _____ units in closed business

Third-Year Yield

16.5% conversion = _____ units in closed business

P - _____

E - _____

C - _____

K - _____

Examples of Prospecting:

_____
_____
_____
_____

Ideas For Staying Top Of Mind:

_____
_____
_____
_____

ACHIEVEMENT
WEEK 12

Congratulations, you're in the final week of T.R.A.C.K.! This week will leave you with more knowledge and increased skill when it comes to converting leads into business. Buckle up and get ready because you are well on your way to being a real estate rock star!

WEEK 12 | ACTIVITIES: CONSISTENCY AND CONVERSION WINS!

WHERE	ACTIVITY	RESOURCE	WORKSHEETS	✓
Task	**IDENTIFY** 5 People to Advance to the Next Stage in Your Pipeline			
Task	**UPDATE** Weekly Calendar	T.R.A.C.K. Workbook	PG 118 - 119	
Task	**HOLD 2** Breakthrough Open Houses	Appendix	PG 124 - 126: Breakthrough Open House Strategies	
Task	**COFFEE OR LUNCH** with at least 2 Core Advocates from your list	Weekly Planner TLR Scripts Booklet		
Task	**MAKE** a minimum of **50** Contacts #TLRTenADay	Activity Tracker TLR Scripts Booklet	PG 117	
Task	**WRITE 10** handwritten notes	Activity Tracker TLR Scripts Booklet	PG 117	
Task	**ADD 15** people to Database	Activity Tracker	PG 117	
Task	**SET 2** new appointments	Activity Tracker	PG 117	
Task	**SHOOT 1** Facebook Live / Instagram video #TLRNation			
Task	**SCRIPT / ROLE PLAY** at least 15 minutes per day	TLR Scripts Booklet		
Online	**WATCH:** Mindset Minute: Consistency Wins Championships (4m)	LockerRoomUniversity.com		
Online	**WATCH & COMPLETE:** All About Converting (21m)	LockerRoomUniversity.com	PG 120: All About Converting	
Challenge	**WEEKLY CHALLENGE:** YOUR Conversion Rates	LockerRoomUniversity.com	PG 120: Your Turn!	
Online	**WATCH:** Congrats! You Did It! Video (4m)	LockerRoomUniversity.com		
Online	**VISIT** The Facebook Group & interact with our community	facebook.com/groups/ LockerRoomNation		
Task	**COMPLETE** Achievement Goal Assessment	T.R.A.C.K. Workbook	PG 121	
Task	**COMPLETE** T.R.A.C.K. Self Assessment	T.R.A.C.K. Workbook	PG 122	

ACTIVITY TRACKER - DATES: _____

	MON	TUES	WED	THURS	FRI	SAT	SUN	ACTUAL	GOAL	TOTAL
ACTIVITIES										
Contacts Made										
Contacts Added to Database										
FSBO Contacts Made										
Expired Contacts Made										
Social Media Contacts Made										
# of Handwritten Notes										
# of Open Houses Held										
# of Doors Knocked										
# of Minutes Script Practicing										
BUSINESS										
Buyer Appointments Held										
Buyer Agency Agreements Signed										
Accepted Buyer Contracts Written										
New Listing Appointments Held										
New Listings Taken										
New Closings From Buyers										
New Closings From Sellers										
Total Closed Volume (Buyer + Seller)										

NOTES / AHA'S

WEEK 12 Calendar

MONDAY _____	TUESDAY _____	WEDNESDAY _____
PRIORITIES	**PRIORITIES**	**PRIORITIES**
1.	1.	1.
2.	2.	2.
3.	3.	3.
6:00AM	6:00AM	6:00AM
7:00AM	7:00AM	7:00AM
8:00AM	8:00AM	8:00AM
9:00AM	9:00AM	9:00AM
10:00AM	10:00AM	10:00AM
11:00AM	11:00AM	11:00AM
12:00AM	12:00AM	12:00AM
1:00PM	1:00PM	1:00PM
2:00PM	2:00PM	2:00PM
3:00PM	3:00PM	3:00PM
4:00PM	4:00PM	4:00PM
5:00PM	5:00PM	5:00PM
6:00PM	6:00PM	6:00PM
7:00PM	7:00PM	7:00PM
8:00PM	8:00PM	8:00PM

CALENDAR HOW TO:

1ST: Personal & Family Time
Date Night, Vacations, Birthdays, etc.

2ND: Events & Other Immovable Things
Lead Gen, Coaching Calls, Trainings, etc.

3RD: Predetermined Appointment Slots
Listing Appts, Showings, Open Houses etc.

4TH: Everything Else
TRACK Activities, Follow up, Transaction Work, Emails, etc.

CURRENT PENDINGS

SELLERS	NOTES / TO DO

BUYERS	NOTES / TO DO

THURSDAY _____	FRIDAY _____	SATURDAY _____
PRIORITIES	**PRIORITIES**	8:00AM
1.	1.	9:00AM
2.	2.	10:00AM
3.	3.	11:00AM
6:00AM	6:00AM	12:00AM
7:00AM	7:00AM	1:00PM
8:00AM	8:00AM	2:00PM
9:00AM	9:00AM	3:00PM
10:00AM	10:00AM	4:00PM
11:00AM	11:00AM	5:00PM
12:00AM	12:00AM	6:00PM
1:00PM	1:00PM	7:00PM
2:00PM	2:00PM	8:00PM
3:00PM	3:00PM	**SUNDAY _____**
4:00PM	4:00PM	8:00AM
5:00PM	5:00PM	9:00AM
6:00PM	6:00PM	10:00AM
7:00PM	7:00PM	11:00AM
8:00PM	8:00PM	12:00AM

MUST DO		
		1:00PM
		2:00PM
		3:00PM
		4:00PM
		5:00PM
		6:00PM
		7:00PM
		8:00PM

ALL ABOUT CONVERSIONS
Time for Some Math

LEADING INDICATORS ➡ _____ ➡ **LAGGING INDICATORS**

MATH TIME!

EXAMPLE: If you went on **100 listing appointments** last year and took a total of **40 listings** for the year, what is your listing appointment to listing taken conversion rate?

Listings Taken ÷ Listing Appointments = Listing Appointment to Listing Taken Conversion Rate

40 ÷ 100 = 40%

WEEKLY CHALLENGE: DIVE INTO YOUR NUMBERS AND CALCULATE YOUR CONVERSION RATES!

YOUR TURN!

Dive into your numbers from the 12 weeks and determine where the opportunities for improvement lie within your conversion rates.

Listing Appointment to Listing Taken (Listings Taken ÷ Listing Appointments)

_____ ÷ _____ = _____%

Listing Taken to Listings Sold (Listings Sold ÷ Listing Taken)

_____ ÷ _____ = _____%

Buyer Appointments to Buyers Agreements Signed (Buyer Agreements Signed ÷ Buyer Appointments)

_____ ÷ _____ = _____%

Buyer Agreements to Buyers Closed (Buyer Closed ÷ Buyer Agreements Signed)

_____ ÷ _____ = _____%

Total Contacts to Total Appointments (Total Appointments ÷ Total Contacts)

_____ ÷ _____ = _____%

CONGRATS! YOU FINISHED THE ACHIEVEMENT SECTION OF T.R.A.C.K.!
ACHIEVEMENT SECTION GOAL ASSESSMENT (WEEKS 10-12)

The goal for the end of the Achievement section was to clearly articulate your story to build the foundation of a referral-based business and create more meaningful relationships, leading to more business and increased conversion rates.

DONE	ACTIVITY
	Created & Shared Your Story Braid
	Established Top of Mind Awareness By Sharing a Market Update Report
	Identified Conversion Rates
	150 Contacts
	45 Contacts Added to Database
	6 Appointments Held
	6 Open Houses Held
	30 Handwritten Notes
	6 Coffee or Lunch Dates with Core Advocates or Preferred Vendors

REFLECT AND WRITE YOUR AHA'S FROM THE ACHIEVEMENT SECTION (WEEKS 10-12):

Hustle & heart set you apart

T.R.A.C.K. PROGRAM SELF ASSESSMENT

After crushing the last 12 weeks, take a look at how far you have come!

	Not Done	Done	Systematized	Mastered
Agent Action Plan Completed and Goals Set	☐	☐	☐	☐
The Amazing Prospecting Race – Achieved at least 40 points	☐	☐	☐	☐
625 Contacts Made	☐	☐	☐	☐
270 Contacts Added to Database	☐	☐	☐	☐
22 Appointments Held	☐	☐	☐	☐
22 Open Houses Held	☐	☐	☐	☐
Perfect Week Implemented	☐	☐	☐	☐
120 Handwritten Notes	☐	☐	☐	☐
2 Top Agents Interviewed	☐	☐	☐	☐
Establish Activity Tracking Habit	☐	☐	☐	☐
Top 50 Core Advocates Identified	☐	☐	☐	☐
Create/Perfect Listing Presentation	☐	☐	☐	☐
Create/Perfect Buyer Consultation	☐	☐	☐	☐
Ideal Client Established	☐	☐	☐	☐
20 Coffee or Lunch Dates with Core Advocates or Preferred Vendors	☐	☐	☐	☐
Sourced Leads and Calculated ROI	☐	☐	☐	☐
Established and Implemented a Follow Up Plan	☐	☐	☐	☐
Planned 12 Month Client Experience Campaign	☐	☐	☐	☐
10 Pop By's Scheduled	☐	☐	☐	☐
Created and Shared Your Story Braid	☐	☐	☐	☐
Established Top of Mind Awareness Plan	☐	☐	☐	☐
Identified Conversion Rates	☐	☐	☐	☐

Make Yourself Proud

APPENDIX
Where all the goods are stashed.

THE TLR BREAKTHROUGH OPEN HOUSE
Countdown to A Successful Sale

5 DAYS BEFORE

Open House Sign or Rider In Yard with Day and Time

Email Blast Open House Flyer to Entire Database

Post to ALL Social Media Platforms

Open House Day & Time Added To All Syndicated Sites
(ie, Zillow, Realtor.com, MLS, etc)

2-3 DAYS BEFORE

Door Knock a Minimum 25 Homes within a 2-3 Block Radium With Flyers

Facebook/Instagram LIVE While Door Knocking

DAY OF

Minimum 4 Directional Arrows/Signs with Balloons at Intersections Leading to Property

Facebook/Instagram LIVE 30 Minutes Before Open House

OPEN HOUSE STRATEGIES
Steps to a Breakthrough Open House

People that tour open houses are raising their hands and telling us they are in the market to buy or sell. Conversion rates at open houses are 25:1 vs. 12:1. You are cutting the time for conversion in half, and converting a cold lead a warm lead. Face to face interaction is the perfect opportunity to build rapport and set an appointment. A successful Open House is where you walk out with AT LEAST ONE, if not 2 or 3 appointments for later that week! ALL YOU NEED is ONE PERSON to say yes to an appointment to consider that Open House a success.

Pro Tip: Do NOT put anyone on an outreach plan for homes unless you have sat down and done a full needs analysis.

MINDSET AFFIRMATIONS

"I am powerful in person."

"I do Open Houses to find clients, not leads."

"There's a client out there looking for me."

"I come from contribution."

"I provide tremendous value to my clients."

SOME PRACTICAL TIPS:

1. If possible, do Open Houses where there is a lot of new development. This allows you to piggy back on the builder's marketing and signage to get traffic to your Open House.

2. Do some research and schedule your Open Houses to be an hour later than everyone else, less competition and could boost traffic in new communities. For example, Sundays 4:00-7:00pm in the summer might be good because new construction offices close at 6:00pm, and you can capture people who will come see you because the sales offices are closed.

3. If you do not have listings, seek out holding Open Houses for other agents who have listings in neighborhoods with homes that have recently gone under contract. This is a signal that the neighborhood is desirable.

4. If the property is another agent's listing, put away all of their marketing materials. This is your Open House.

5. Leave nothing out, except your Open House binder and sign in sheet/clipboard with a few pens. If they have the info and their nose buried in a flyer or info sheet, they have no need to interact with you.

6. Invest in a large quantity of signs
   - Design your sign so that your name is in a large print size
   - Brand your name. Put your name on all signs, including directional signs
   - Always use colorful balloons
   - Place 10+ signs out (check local city ordinances)
   - Put out signs five days before open house date (check local city ordinances)

7. Ask neighbors with corner lots to place signs on their property (check local city ordinances)
   - Place directional signs at key turns, (check local city ordinances)
   - Put your phone number on the hanging sign on open house lawn

TIME BLOCK OPEN HOUSE ACTIVITIES
Stay Organized and on Track

BEFORE

ACTIVITY	TIME	DAY OF THE WEEK
Choose House to Hold Open	10 minutes	
Coach Sellers About Preparations and Staging	20 minutes	
Design Marketing/Ads/Fliers	1 hour	
Update MLS/Listing Sites with Open House Information	1/2 hour	
Post to Your Facebook/Instagram Business Pages	1/2 hour	
Put out 6–10 signs	1 hour	
Email Database	1/2 hour	
Prepare Packets	1 hour	
Door Knock Neighborhood & Facebook LIVE	2 hours	
Place Sign/Rider in Yard	10 minutes	
Directional Signs at Intersection (minimum 4)	1/2 hour	

DURING

ACTIVITY	TIME	DAY OF THE WEEK
Directional Signs at Intersections (Min. 4 if not permitted before the day of the Open House)	1/2 hour	
Facebook LIVE when you arrive (do not do a walk through of the house)	10 minutes	
Facebook LIVE at the end (reminder to schedule showings to see if they missed out)	5 minutes	

AFTER

ACTIVITY	TIME	DAY OF THE WEEK
Follow Up with Seller	10 minutes	
Add New Leads to Database	1 hour	
Follow Up with Leads (Call, Text, Email)	1-2 hours	

TOP AGENT INTERVIEW QUESTIONS
Learn From the Best

THANK THEM FIRST *"Thank you so much for giving me 30 minutes of your time to ask you questions. I believe success leaves clues and when I was challenged to think of someone that I want to model my business after, I immediately thought of you. It really means a lot that you'd be willing to dedicate your time to help me and I hope I can pay it forward to someone else in the future."*

QUESTIONS:

- If you don't mind, please tell me about your current business production… (Sales Volume, Units Closed, Team Structure if applicable, yearly goals vs actuals)
- What did you do prior to real estate? And why did you get into real estate?
- Based on your reason for getting into real estate, on a scale of 1-10 how would you rank yourself in regards to fulfilling the original purpose? (Pertaining to financial goals, flexibility, running own business, freedom)
- In your first two years of business, what were the key lead generation activities you did to earn business?
- Outside of Lead Generation, what was the most important thing you did in your first two years to build your business?
- Looking back and knowing what you know now, what would you have done differently?
- What advice do you wish someone would have given you while launching your business?
- How long would you say it took before you started to see your business hit momentum so it began to generate referral business? What would you say was the key trigger to cause that?
- What is an example of when you "failed" but were able to use it as a defining moment in your career to propel you to where you are today? What did you learn from that failure?
- Did you ever have reluctance to ask people for business? How did you overcome it?
- How do you manage expectations with clients so you are able to balance personal life and work life?
- What is the biggest mistake you see most agents make early on in their career?
- What would you say your "expertise" is when it comes to lead generation that leads to your primary source of business? Can you tell me about that and how you've mastered it?
- What is your answer if someone asks why they should work with you vs. another agent?
- How do you go about time blocking so you stick to your calendar in order to balance lead generation, open houses, negotiating contracts, along with all of the training and other demands?
- Who holds YOU accountable to your goals and why is accountability so important for you in obtaining your goals?
- What is the biggest piece of advice you'd give an agent like me who is seeking to grow their business the same way you have?
- What does the next level of success look like to you?

SELLER LEAD SHEET

	LEAD SOURCE:
Name:	Name:
Phone:	Phone:
Email:	Email:

Property Address:		
City:	State:	Zip:

How long have you owned this home? When did you purchase this property?
Where are you moving to? Why are you selling this property?
How soon do you need to be there?
What are your plans if the property does not sell?
If you were a buyer looking to purchase your HOUSE today, what would you pay for it?
How much do you currently owe on your property?
Is anyone else involved in the selling decision?
Tell me a little about your home especially any upgrades you have done:

Bedrooms:	Baths:	Garage:	Basement:

BONUS: On a scale of 1-10 with 10 being your home is perfect, how would you rate it? What would make it a 10?
When I come over on _____ are you prepared to list with me at that time?
Will all decision makers be present for the appointment?
Other things I need to know? (Divorce/Estate/Income Property)

BUYER LEAD SHEET

	LEAD SOURCE:		
Name:	Name:		
Phone:	Phone:		
Email:	Email:		
Current address:			
City:	State:		Zip:
Do you currently rent or own?			
Do you need to sell your current property before you can buy?			
How soon do you want to be settled into your new home?			
Will you be financing or paying cash?			
What is your price range?			
Are you Pre-approved?/Have you met with a lender?			
If Yes: Lenders Name:		Mortgage Company:	
Is anyone else involved in the purchasing decision?			
Tell me about the home you are looking for?			
Bedrooms:	Baths:	Garage:	Other:
If I found you the perfect home and it needed paint and new flooring would you be interested?			
On a scale of 1-10 with 10 being you want to buy a home today, where would you rate yourself?			
What would it take to make it a 10?			
NOTES			

CONTRIBUTOR BIOS
Team Members Who Helped Create This Incredible Game Plan

BRENT SCOTT

Brent is an Area Expansion Director with The Locker Room. Soon after beginning his real estate career in 2003, Brent quickly identified his passion for agent development. When asked in 2017 to create a coaching program in his office of 230+ agents, Brent turned to The Locker Room for guidance, support, and leverage. Since then, Brent has helped dozens of real estate coaches and company leaders grow their office coaching and development programs. Throughout his coaching career, Brent's focus has evolved. After vetting the needs of offices across the country, Brent now focuses his efforts on assisting real estate leaders across the Gulf States in creating a culture of development within their organizations by leveraging The Locker Room's world-class tools, systems, and resources to propel the success of the blue ocean agents everywhere.

JAKE DIXON

As a former college and professional baseball player, Jake has brought his passion for coaching and building championship winning teams to the real estate game. Jake was the CEO of major real estate offices for a number of years which were top-ranked nationally. Through his leadership experience, he found his true passion for coaching and serving others so he could help other people achieve the same success. The Locker Room was founded in 2016 and has partnered with hundreds of real estate brokerages and real estate coaches along with serving thousands of real estate agents across the Nation. Jake is married to Carissa who helps run the day to day operations of the business and they have two daughters. In his spare time, Jake enjoys spending time with his family, playing with his dogs, and being outdoors fishing and searching for Native American Indian artifacts to add to his collection.

JENNIFER HENRY

An accomplished coach for real estate agents and brokers, Jennifer's average agent client will make $300,000 and will sell about 30 units. While she is a Certified Professional and Executive Coach, she gained all her experience from the vast array of roles held inside the real estate industry. From single agent to a team member to team leader, to productivity coach to broker...over the last 17 years, she's experienced the industry from almost every angle. She understands what it takes to make a real career that provides an income worthy of the time and effort it requires. Her passion is to help real estate agents have all that they dream is possible while also enjoying a full and balanced life. This drive is why she calls herself a "Life Coach for Real Estate Professionals"!

Your Vibe Attracts Your Tribe

JENNIFER TAYLOR

Jennifer is an 18+ year real estate veteran. Her career includes Managing Broker, VP of Career Development, Team Leader, and Productivity Coach, all while running her own sales business. Coaching and developing leaders is her passion. "I find great pleasure developing others and seeing them achieve their goals, even more seeing them go beyond what they set out to accomplish. I love to crunch numbers, develop a plan to improve the bottom line, and help put the wheels in motion." - Jennifer

LEONNA WEISS

Leonna is the Broker/Owner of Weiss Choice Realty. Since she started her real estate career in 2015, she has sold a career volume of $67.7mm in 5 years by helping over 230 buyers/sellers with their real estate needs. She has done all of this on her own, with the exception of her trusted executive assistant. Leonna achieved a plethora of awards as a real estate agent, including being named #1 agent in the Carolina Region for volume in 2019. Repeatedly ranked in the top 10 individual agents in NC/SC Region, Leonna is published in Triangle Real Producers Magazine, listed in the Triangle Business Journal for Top 25 Producing Individual agents, and has earned various awards within her brokering firm.

Outside of real estate, you can catch her working out at 5 am (it's the only time she can fit it in) or spending time with her four kids. Leonna tries to make sure she's available to drop off/pick up from school and attend as many sports/school events as possible. "I'm working on creating a 'net life' and not just focusing on the next closing. It's essential not to lose sight of what's important." - Leonna

MARK SIMPSON

Mark Simpson is a real estate agent, Associate Broker and Director of Productivity with Keller Williams Flowood, MS. Mark has served as the Team Leader/CEO of KW Flowood and the General Manager of multiple KW Market Centers in the state of Louisiana.

Before real estate, Mark was a therapist and life coach for twenty-two years and created Marathon Makeover, a 40-week wellness program that turned over 4,000 couch potatoes into marathoners. He is a husband, father of three daughters, grandfather to two grandchildren, and eight-time marathon finisher.

NATHAN DANIEL

Finding your niche and growing your legacy into something meaningful and profitable is the goal of Nathan Daniel. With a resume including Southwest Regional Director, business development coach, real estate agent, and former team leader, he knows his stuff. Nathan strives to inspire his clients to become their best selves while teaching them the essential skills they need to build an empire in their lives that will leave a lasting legacy. He began his real estate career in 2009, successfully building a business designed around relationships with his clients. Through these relationships and follow up systems, Nathan began to find his passion for teaching others to work hard and achieve their goals. As a young entrepreneur, starting his first business when he was only 14 years old, Nathan has developed and cultivated the values he now exhibits as he strives to impact and empower his clients, family, friends, and community.

Imperfect Action Beats Inaction... Every Time!

Made in the USA
Columbia, SC
21 February 2021